FEB 16, 1988

Alan & Marsha,

This book is very special. I hope it is as valueable to you guys as it was for us.

Love
Scott

THE SILVER CORD

THE SILVER CORD

Lifeline to the Unobstructed

Marti Barham, R.N., Ph.D.

&

Tom Greene, Ph.D.

DeVorss & Co.
P.O. Box 550
Marina del Rey, CA 90294-550

ISBN: 0-87516-562-1

Library of Congress Card Catalog Number:
85-63215

Printed in the United States of America

To Aenka and Mario

for their presence, interest, and assistance

Contents

Foreword

To read this book is to embark on a journey into controversial areas of knowledge that could strongly challenge some basic value and/or belief systems. While the subject areas and information represented here are very diversified, I believe the authors have carefully and deliberately avoided distortion and present the data clearly.

In a very real sense, the book is an open invitation to delve into some aspects of the profound meaningfulness of life. Should any part appear mysterious, I am sure it will yield to your own personal exploration and individual evaluation. Whether you peruse casually or read it with careful concentration, I hope you will keep an open mind.

I have known Drs. Barham and Greene for some years. They are excellent teachers as well as being accomplished eclectic therapists. When I have worked with them individually or together, the impact has always been refreshingly stimulating. I believe they have succeeded admirably in maintaining that effect in this volume of information sharing.

CARLTON DUCKWORTH, M.D.

Introduction

Where it is a duty to worship the sun it is pretty sure to be a crime to examine the laws of heat.

Pratably from "Bartletts Quotations —Voltaire
P641

Man's search for meaning and purpose in life beyond physical maintenance and personal gratification is doubtlessly older than recorded history. Archaeological and anthropological research routinely turns up evidence of this search across both centuries and cultures. It appears to be a universal finding that man develops various theories and beliefs regarding how and why this earth and its inhabitants came to be. Explanations based on these beliefs vary from culture to culture, but prior to the current scientific period the basic conclusions were the same: unseen forces shape worlds and beings; life in some form continues after physical death.[1] Most religions teach some type of organizing form of consciousness or God, and that life in some form continues after death. Throughout history, many persons have described spiritual experiences that attest to such beliefs.

"Explaevations" are just that: they usually exfout the plain facts!

"Conclusions" are assumptions and to assume anything only makes an ("assume") ars out of you + me!

And we must to look at "teaching" eg. what was and is "conditioning or teaching from birth then left must dis with a lot & excess baggage to get rid of."

xi

It has become popular during the last fifty years or so for many scientific researchers to use the concept of "creation myths" in explaining these beliefs and experiences. This viewpoint holds that the basic "truth" behind these beliefs and experiences is that mankind simply does not want to accept its mortality. Man is said to create fanciful myths to salve his ego in an attempt to deny physical mortality and to account for otherwise unknown facts of life and death. Perhaps such researchers are themselves doing what they interpret others to be doing and in their own lack of understanding look to an acceptable psychological explanation that fits known data and accounts for their own ignorance.[2]

A similar interpretive attitude has been taken toward a phenomenon called the *near-death experience*. This usually powerful experience is often described as spiritual or transcendent, frequently resulting in a dramatic increase in a person's belief in life after death.[3] This phenomenon has yet to be adequately explained by known medical or psychological processes, although some rigorous attempts have been made.[4]

A typically cautious scientific attitude regarding near-death and similar subjective experiences is expressed by Richard Blacher, M.D. "We are dealing here with the fantasy of death . . . it establishes the certainty of heaven, where one can have a reunion with people from the past, and where one can have a life after death. That it answers so many puzzles of mankind and creates a bridge between science and religion makes it a tempting concept for speculation. It is for this very reason that the physician must be especially wary of accepting religious belief as scientific data."[5]

Michael Sabom, M.D., whose professional opinion regarding the reality of the near-death experience was changed after his own researches, responded in a rebuttal to this paper that "equal caution should be exercised in accepting scientific belief as scientific data."[6] Dr. Sabom is cogently pointing to the fact that beliefs can work either way and that scientific belief is worth no more than popular belief until adequate data are gathered.

experience makes it so for me. (I)

We believe it is important to have a "least limiting" point of view in the search for explanations to life and its meaning. One such point of view that seems just as sensible as the creation-myth hypothesis and yet provides a broader theoretical basis for investigation might be considered a spiritual one. This orientation proposes that there is purpose to life, that life is not mere accident nor is it limited to strictly physical events as we have learned to measure them. As the word is used today, a *spiritual* viewpoint assumes that the sheer magnitude of life-after-death beliefs— evidenced in books, sermons, meditations, wondering, art forms in all of recorded history—reflects a real spark of memory and the desire to reconnect with "something" we somehow feel and know *is* there.

The pursuit of the knowledge of creation and the mysteries of possible nonphysical life, with all the aspects of physical living such knowledge would imply, touches the life of everyone. Who of us has not had some experience(s) we considered spiritual or religious? No matter that, like quicksilver, it may have slipped away. What does matter is that for howsoever long or short a period, we had some sense of understanding, some feeling of identity with others, some glimpse of purpose to our lives other than physical maintenance and self-gratification. We believe that each adult continues the search for a meaning to life, even though at times we may not be active in our search. *I hope so!*

Those who have been in touch with what they consider a spiritual experience refer often to an inner peace, an inner knowing, and to having a bit more balance or perspective in their experience of life. Such people may be said in a sense to have come face to face with a reflection of their soul and, through that reflection, to have perhaps experienced a glimpse of God. Unfortunately, many open themselves to a spiritual experience only to interpret it and categorize it in a manner familiar to themselves and accepted by others, but one that may not be very growth-producing. The tendency to seek familiar structure in an attempt intellectually to understand unique and powerful experiences seems unavoidable. At least to the extent that we are shaped by our culture and language, we attempt to use known data to explain unknown phenomena. *true*

Word pictures and explanations of many seers, sages, and religious leaders have been passed down for generations. Who has not read, or listened to, an acknowledged religious or spiritual authority speaking of God and what life is about? In childhood, as one listens and understands literally, thoughts and ideas are formulated that form a *context* for a *concept* of God. For those adults who pray, the early word pictures created during the literal and concrete-minded growth period of childhood often return. When the need or urge for answers to deeper questions of the meaning of life moves us as adults, we typically look for religious structures that seem not only most appropriate but also most familiar. *Some need "something" more universal.*

Formal religion initially offered supportive structures for understanding and for individual spiritual growth, as religion was originally intended as a *vehicle* through which man could be in touch with the spiritual aspect within.[7] Early churches offered a physically safe place, association with others seeking similar information or experience, solace, leaders who showed compassion for man's plight, and meaningful rituals. Rituals have always offered social man an opportunity for experiences that foster a shared sense of commonality, a feeling of connectedness with others, a natural and positive high, and, at times, a mystical experience.

Unfortunately, orthodox religions now too often fall short of providing meaningful structure and experiential awareness as well as viable information. Through the years Christian religions in particular have mostly changed for the worse. Many Christian denominations focus on fear and guilt, seeking to instill a belief in a vengeful or vindictive Creator and an all-devouring Satan. Others have rigid hierarchies and inflexible rules that leave people feeling "less than" or stupid rather than uplifted and informed. Clergy have often set themselves apart, and over thousands of years there has been an increasing emphasis on money and the church's power to determine for other individuals how they should feel and behave. Sin and guilt effectively now form the basis for Western religion. Divisiveness among different factions has occurred to the point that some claim to be the "only way" and clearly or subtly damn all others to a supposed hell. The church has come to be an *end unto itself* rather than a *means whereby*.

Contemporary man is not only finding his childhood or parental church less supportive and satisfying than he would like—he is bombarded by extensive media information concerning many different approaches to the spiritual search. Within the context of a crumbling religious support system, he is thus faced with many alternatives in his individual search. While at first such a confused picture might appear dreary, this is not really the case. Given the state of current Western religion, such a challenge is as much an asset as a liability. It will ultimately influence a person to look for his own truth. One of the thrusts of this volume is, in fact, that a spiritual search *is* essentially an individual search; and that while a formal structure might be helpful, the crucial elements are the attitude, orientation, beliefs, and behavior of each of us as individuals.

What is this elusive and multifaceted quality we call *spiritual* for which man so yearns? The authors of this book believe spirituality to be the manifestation of a real and natural part of each human being, that part of us that is our soul. A soul is a reality, not an idea—a God-given gift to ensure our completeness as well as to serve His purposes. A soul is a tiny facet of Him, a divine spark that suffuses us and serves as our link to Him. Our spiritual aspect gives us an inborn push towards the pursuit of our Creator, a pursuit that through the centuries has been a reflection of our individual inner search.

This spiritual aspect is as natural as our other three major human aspects—physical, emotional, and intellectual. Our physical apparatus interacts with the world and sustains physical life. Our emotional aspect supplies us with feelings and natural emotional responses that give depth and breadth to our existence. Our intellectual aspect provides us with the ability to reason and *As you think, so shall your powers + blessings be.* meet challenges in living. Our spiritual aspect ensures individual uniqueness in our approach to life and continuation after physical death. It is these four aspects, not politics or chance, that make us all created equal. *They are having a lot. of fun trying to control/ rather than just Being!*

It is our spiritual aspect that gives us access to psychic awareness and constructive intuition and that also increases our awareness of subtle influences from nonphysical sources. This aspect enables us to have the powerful subjective experiences frequently associated with spirituality. Unfortunately, as a result of distortions in mankind's patterns of living that have occurred over thousands of years, contemporary man's awareness of his spiritual aspect has dimmed. Many thousands of years ago man was much more in touch with his spiritual aspect than he is now. Mankind has strayed far from a healthier, rhythmic form of living based on a balanced use of his four basic dimensions. Indeed, it is now difficult for many to experience direct contact with their spiritual aspect at all. *This depends on who the "many" are.*

Many people believe that spirituality and spiritual experiences lie outside physical life. The authors disagree. Spirituality encompasses *all* aspects of our life, both in and out of the body. It is a combined or integrated experience of attitude, awareness, feelings of appreciation and humility. It involves a willingness to learn, with a focus on the development of unconditional love. Within man there exists a continuous process directed towards integrating all feelings and attitudes into constructive and positive behavior for ourselves and our fellow man. *Con be directed - but it is not automatic.*

Spirituality, while we are in the body, is thus not only inner awareness and subjective experience but use of our spiritual aspect in daily life. As one of the authors' teachers put it, "There have been many questions regarding spirituality and what it is. It is everything—everything combined with something else. It is a rhythmic combination of all the checks and balances of life."

Why don't the "authors" use religions + now how to love beings in uncondition seeking.

Historians and social commentators have clearly documented the age of intellectual enlightenment in cognitive and scientific directions. We fly in the skies, we peer at creatures from the deepest ocean depths, we view planets far distant from earth. We have passed from personal belief to measurable data as a basis for operational truths. Yet, who we are individually or collectively other than pieces of productive protoplasm remains a mystery. Perhaps now that we have "conquered" our physical environment and see the unity of that which we are on the verge of destroying, we are ready once again to ponder the mystery of life on a personal basis.

The imbalance of contemporary industrial society is making it progressively easier for people to see man's collective self-destruct course. We suspect it is not an accident that in recent years publications on spiritual and psychic subjects have increased. While many observers point to this as an escape from the dehumanizing aspects of our busy and technological society, some believe otherwise. Marilyn Ferguson's The Aquarian Conspiracy[8] offers a description of similar changes in attitudinal thinking that appear to be developing in many areas of study and research.

This book presents information that the authors have obtained about man's individual spiritual journey and about mankind's collective spiritual struggle. It would be unfair and inaccurate to present the contents as originating with the authors, for it did not. The information was offered to them after a period of many years' experimentation in psychic and spiritual directions, primarily through the efforts of Marti Barham and her husband, Jay, a minister. Tom Greene became involved in these efforts in 1980.

Initial contact with unknown forces or energies came via the discovery and development of Jay's psychic ability around 1957. This evolved into experiments with trance states and eventually Jay's ability to function as a voice channel, or what is sometimes called a trance medium. Essentially this is a process in which someone sensitive to his spiritual/psychic aspects goes into an altered state of consciousness, often referred to as a trance. The belief is that this human channel is able to set his or her personality largely aside and allow some discarnate intelligence to use his/her body and apparatus as a vehicle for communication.⁹ Frequently the information relates to subjects of which the channel has no prior or conscious knowledge. While the information gained via voice channeling was impressive and seemed consistent, Jay and Marti knew that this process was at most 80 percent accurate. There is apparently always some unintentional distortion in voice channeling by the personality, values, biases, or emotional blind spots of the channel.

By the late 1960s Jay, Marti, and a group of fellow experimenters had been told via voice channeling that the intelligences they were in contact with were discarnate souls of people who had previously lived on earth. A decision was made in 1971 to attempt direct voice contact with these beings in hopes of diminishing or eliminating the distortions of voice channeling. After several years of experimenting, what appeared to be physical materialization was achieved. Bodies began to form with discernible voices.

Eventually Jay and Marti, along with others who had joined them in their group efforts, were fairly consistently experiencing the presence of what appeared to be partially or fully materialized beings who identified themselves as "entities." The most widely used name for these beings in popular and spiritual literature would be *spirit guides, spirits*, or simply *guides*. The group began to call their channeling sessions *darkrooms*, since they met in a darkened room.

The entities initially contacted gradually accustomed the group participants to their presence. They worked patiently and slowly to provide a wide variety of nonfrightening physical and psychic phenomena as evidence of their existence and as a way of easing the many fears of the group members. Most participants' fears seemed to focus either on personal psychological fears or religious/spiritual fears regarding evil spirits, Satan, "lower souls," and the like. Once the majority of the group had enough personal evidence of the apparent reality of this incredible phenomenon and had reduced their fears considerably, the entities began a combination of teaching and counseling along both psychological and spiritual lines. Those who remained unconvinced of the reality of the phenomena, or who were unable to reduce their fear of the unknown to tolerable levels, were never given a "sales pitch" by either the other group members or the entities. Each person was encouraged by the entities to believe what felt most true to him and that with which he was most comfortable. Some elected to leave the group, but many remained.

There were a rather large number of entities who visited with the group at one time or another, but two in particular evolved into frequent visitors and consistent teachers. They identified themselves as Aenka and Mario, and the group has had many sessions with them. The material presented in this book is almost exclusively from them. Aenka was initially the more frequent visitor, but in the last several years he has been less active, and Mario has appeared more often. While the teaching and interaction styles of each are quite different, the material they present seems identical. Indeed, as we worked on typed transcripts of tape-recorded sessions stretching over six years, their comments could be intermingled freely without losing any continuity or thrust. While individual statements would be phrased differently, and both seemed to have different emphases reflecting their different personalities, the teachings seemed cut of the same cloth.

Aenka (pronounced *ángka*) appears as a Black. He is usually quite tall and always speaks with a definite well-educated British-type accent. His voice is deep; he speaks slowly and with much care in his choice of words. Somehow, even though it is apparent that he cares greatly for mankind, he remains a bit aloof and distant in his contacts.

Mario is quite a contrast. He appears as a Caucasian, shorter that Aenka, claiming to have been Italian in his last physical lifetime. His accent could probably best be described as mixed middle European. His voice is not as deep as Aenka's, but it is stronger. He speaks with more audible clarity, and his speech is more rapid than Aenka's. While he too can be distant and cool, Mario often laughs and makes provocative jokes or statements. While Aenka elicits quiet respect from most participants, Mario can push emotional buttons that at times generate strong feelings.

For the authors to claim that they believe this materialization phenomenon to be real would be, of course, an incredible statement. We certainly have no intention of attempting to "prove" the experience as real to anyone. That would be impossible, in view of the fact that a number of scientific minds have for a long time been attempting to "prove" the validity of much simpler psychic phenomena, such as precognition, telekinesis, clairvoyance, and what is called poltergeist activity.[10] Despite some very convincing data stretching over many years from all parts of the world, the scientific community is by and large convinced that such things cannot occur. We would, however, like to offer you a bit of information about ourselves, both by way of getting acquainted and for helping you estimate our credibility.

Marti Barham is a registered nurse with an M.S. in rehabilitation counseling and a Ph.D. in psychology. She is licensed as a registered nurse in several states and as a marriage and family counselor in California. She is also certified as a disability examiner, rehabilitation counselor, sex therapist, and alcohol/drug abuse counselor. Her background also includes extensive experience in psychiatric nursing. She has been in private counseling practice since 1974. From 1977 to June 1981 she and her husband, Jay, were associated with Elisabeth Kübler-Ross and participated in all of her Life/Death/Transition workshops during that period. Presently, in addition to her involvement in several types of community services, Marti maintains a part-time independent practice in Merced, California. She is a member of the American Association of Marriage and Family Counselors; the American Association of Sex Educators, Counselors, and Therapists; the National Rehabilitation Counseling Association; Counselors on Alcoholism, Addictions and Related Dependencies; the National Association of

Alcoholism Counselors; the Alcohol and Drug Problems Association of North America; and the California Association of Alcoholism Counselors. She and Jay have been married for twenty-six years and have an adult son. Believing strongly in the effectiveness of personal therapy, she has involved herself in much personal growth work as well as facilitating the growth of others.

Tom Greene holds a Ph.D. in clinical psychology, is licensed to practice psychology in Hawaii, and has for fourteen years been in independent practice, with previous inpatient and outpatient staff experience. He is a member of the American Psychological Association; the Hawaii Psychological Association; the American Academy of Psychotherapists, and the International Association of Near Death Studies. He has been married for thirteen years and is a father and stepfather. He has also had considerable personal therapy.

While the idea of physical materialization is difficult to conceive of, and even more difficult to consider as a possible reality, such reports are not new. Religious and secular history is filled with accounts of visions of, and encounters with, beings from another plane of existence. Materialization phenomena have been studied more or less scientifically for at least one hundred years along with a more stringently tested variety of psychic phenomena during the past forty years.[11] The reader interested in the authors' direct experiences is referred to Marti's first book, *Bridging Two Worlds*,[12] a personal documentary of the development of the group sessions from which this material is drawn. It includes much anecdotal and evidential data to support the subjective reality of our experience, a number of firsthand accounts by participants, and some selected quotations from the entities.

Our purpose in presenting the information in this book is simply to share it. To repeat: we have no desire to attempt to *prove* the validity of the teachings or the reality of our experiences. We have found the personal experiences in our meetings very meaningful and constructive, and for us the spiritual teachings have *a conclusion is a closing, a decision by reasoning rather than experience.*

been profound and consistent. Rather than trying to persuade others to believe our experiences, we share the entities' attitude of leaving people to reach their own conclusions.

The present material consists of direct quotations from the entities and the authors' paraphrases or summation of their comments and statements. While some of these paraphrases may seem interpretive, this is not the case. The attitudes and opinions expressed are those of the entities, not the authors. Statements are made authoritatively and are presented as what the entities gave as facts. The authors ask the reader to bear in mind this manner of presentation, the purpose of which is clarity of expression in conveying the entities' information. To qualify each statement, referencing it to supportive or nonsupportive published works, would be a herculean task. The goal of the form and style is to present the material in a straightforward manner. However, since many aspects of the information overlap and interweave, we have in some chapters organized the materials into subsections for clarity of presentation as well as for emphasis of key aspects. Some references and chapter notes are included as possible sources of published material the authors find interesting. We use the word *man* as representing both individual men and women; no sexism is implied.

CHAPTER ONE

The Soul, the Source, and the Three Universes

*The decisive question for man is: is he related to something in-
finite or not? That is the telling quesion of his life. Only if we
can know the thing which truly matters is the Infinite can we
avoid fixing our interest upon futility.* *And we can
only know through experience.* —Carl Jung

DEFINITIONS AND OVERVIEW

Each of us has a soul, a spiritual aspect every bit as real as our
physical aspect. We cannot identify it directly with our physical
senses nor have we learned to detect it technologically, but it is
there and it is not a wisp of smoke. It is a form of organized energy and exists just as surely as did electrical or magnetic energy
before we discovered their presence.[1]

Souls are created by God, also referred to as the Source, or
Source of All Divinity, and indeed are tiny facets *of* the Source.
Unlike our physical aspect, the soul never dies; once given birth, it
lives forever. Our souls are very purposeful in their individual and

1

collective evolution, and the end of their journey is merging once again with God. At this ultimate destination of returning to our spiritual Father/Mother we blend with the Source and yet retain our uniqueness as we add our tiny bit to that which is the Source. Once created, it is impossible for a soul not to return. It may take many lifetimes in physical bodies to gather all the learning experiences that will characterize our completeness and uniqueness, but all souls *will get back*. To ensure this, the Source created a fail-safe design. This chapter provides an overview of that design, while subsequent chapters describe some of its many aspects.

To form a frame of reference enabling you to picture our souls as they move in and out of physical bodies on earth, as well as the relationship of all souls to the Source, it is necessary to refer to what the entities with whom we have been in contact call the *three universes*. "There are in all of the heavens, what you would call in all space or in all matter, three universes: the obstructed universe which is the physical; the unobstructed universe; and the Source of All Divinity."*

The obstructed universe is the physical universe as we know it. Our awareness of it is through our physical senses and technological aids to our senses. The unobstructed universe is that universe where our soul (the spiritual essence or entity within us) dwells between and after lives in the physical body. In this book we will use the terms *entity* and *soul* interchangeably.

The unobstructed universe is not usually available to us through our physical senses, but we can be in touch with it in other ways that will be described later. The unobstructed universe is the current home of the entities that we are in contact with in our darkroom sessions, according to their statement. The Source's universe, the beginning and end of everything, is in a general sense that universe usually referred to as *heaven*.

*Unless otherwise noted, all quotations are verbatim as given by the entities and taken from transcriptions of audiotaped darkroom sessions.

This is the impingement in the reference of many prophets and wise men who have closely identified this. The universe of the Source of All Divinity is exactly what they are trying to spell out, trying to identify. It is completion and is the heavenly body that is the height of pleasure.

Most of us brought up in a Western/European religious and scientific culture are oriented to the concepts of three-dimensional space and linear time. God and angels are typically depicted as being "up there" and heaven as being some type of more or less physical place. However, the entities speak of the three universes as *literally coexisting*, operating simultaneously but with different types and frequencies of energies. For entities in the unobstructed, time and space have very different meanings than for us in the obstructed universe.[2]

You live in the obstructed. I live in the unobstructed. When you see the universe it is dimensioned, due to the behavior of physical energy. The primary difference in any energy is the — frequency with which it functions. Imagine yourself and everything else being encapsulated into one dome filled with three energies—physical, psychic and spiritual—all functioning on their own frequency, simultaneously. Each independent, and also interdependent, but not interfering with one another.

The three general energy types Mario (one of the entities described in the Introduction) refers to in the above statement roughly correspond to the three universes. Physical energy is the energy of the obstructed universe, i.e. the one with which we are familiar and can measure. It is initially created and set into evolutionary motion by the Source, and once set into motion, it takes its predetermined course with its own laws of consistency, change, and gradual evolution. Psychic energy is described as a "free energy" that permeates the three universes. It is used as a literal binding agent for physical and spiritual energy and can be used as a communication link between and within the universes. Spiritual energy derives directly from the Source, suffuses all three universes, and cannot be consciously manipulated by man.

These three energies are always functioning and do so independently of one another even though there are a variety of types of interaction between them. Each was designed for certain purposes and to be capable of operating by itself. However, in order for the energies to be capable of *continuing* to function and best serve their multiple purposes, they must act in an interdependent fashion.

> Each energy has certain independence and dependence, even though there is interdependence. Everything and all things require a source of energy, without which it becomes depleted. These energies are interdependent in that spiritual energy is dependent on psychic energy and physical energy to replenish each survival, expansion, or evolvement. There is nothing perpetual; there must be a replenishing, a nurturing.

It is not hard to imagine physical energies needing to interact for their own continuation or to produce an altered energy form or product. Oxygen and hydrogen need to combine to produce water; we need air for breathing in order to sustain our bodies; man needs woman for procreation and vice versa; children and parents experience mutual benefit from interaction; and so on. Nor is it very hard to imagine psychic and physical energy being dependent on the Source's universe, since that universe is the beginning and end of all things. It is somewhat more difficult to imagine how the Source or Its energy depends upon anything but itself. If the Source is the beginning and end of all things, how could it possibly need anything other than itself? Mario couched his response to this question in the context of a simple and rather earthy comparison, as he often does when the authors have trouble understanding.

It is very similar to vinegar and oil that is used for salad dressing. Each one is independent, but interdependent in that the combined effect is needed to reach an objective. Physical energy would serve no purpose without spiritual energy. Spiritual energy could not carry out its processes without psychic and physical energy. Each type has its own specific function or responsibility, and they work independently in an interdependent relationship. They are very much the same as the social structure of man wherein independence and dependence form interdependence.

In this sense God may be thought of as indeed being dependent on other forms of energy, as well as on man, to expand and carry out Its mission.[3]

Mario also spoke of spiritual energy as dependent on physical energy in reference to individual souls and the spiritual energy contained in them. "Spiritual energy is dependent upon physical energy and your physical body for a housing, a castle, for the soul which is your spirit. The Source is dependent upon this agent to offer the soul experiences that are necessary. Spiritual energy is bound to the physical upon entry of the soul into a body. It cannot leave the physical body permanently, or have total separation from it, until the death of the physical form." He made a rough comparison of the soul being dependent on the body to a very mundane event. "It is similar in a general manner to your being dependent upon your car or some other vehicle to go on a journey. Somewhat you are dependent upon that mode of transportation because you could not have those experiences without your vehicle."

Spiritual energy is dependent upon psychic energy since "psychic energy is the connecting force that causes a marriage of physical and spiritual energy, that form of energy which maintains the relationship between the soul and the physical body. This relates to what has been called the *silver cord*."

The three coexisting universes and types of energies provide the context or background for the emergence of individual souls from the Source and for their challenging journey back to the Source. But what of the Source itself?

> The great Source of Divinity is all there is and all there ever will be. It has caused everything to be and it will continue to cause everything to exist. God, your Father, is that of which you were born. As a Facet of Divinity you were born into and from the Source, and to the Source, the Father, you will return. I cannot offer you any insight on what it is like in the universal Source of All Divinity. I can only tell you that it is the all powerful and it is home.

The authors were surprised to learn the entities could say relatively little directly or specifically of the Source. Just as we in the obstructed have limitations in our direct contact with entities in the unobstructed, they also have limitations in their direct experience of God and His universe. "It is as difficult for us in the unobstructed to communicate with the Source as it is for you to communicate with us. The Source is an impenetrable field of energy that you are not permitted to enter until you have completed your destiny. You can visit and explore the perimeter. You can be aware of some aspects past the barrier, and communicate through the field; but you cannot enter." When asked what it was like to be at the edge of that field, Mario responded quite simply, "It is magnificent."

One evening Aenka (another entity described in the Introduction) apparently anticipated the classical question of where the Source itself came from.

> And you will be asking the question, where did it all start? Where did God come from? How could something begin out of nothing? Man will not know that, you only learn those things when you move back to the Source. There is always, in the progression of evolution and growth, something to look

forward to. That will be the dessert of the efforts of evolution. And if one needs to be so arrogant as to dwell on those unattainable facts then they only limit their understanding and growth in what they are permitted to understand.[4]

Why does the Source create and manipulate physical energy, set evolutionary processes in motion, and create souls to be sent on an incredible journey of learning? *There is no answer to a "why" question!*

For the contributions to the Source, upon merging. This assists the evolutionary growth process. If you would take your own culture back a million years ago, it was very primitive, was it not? It had far less then the capabilities it has now scientifically. This has escalated because of expanded knowledge and the experiences that are continuing to be returned to the Source. And from that Source there is rebirth of new entities who continue to add to the strength and the knowledge and the power. The Source itself continues to grow and as this evolution continues the Source becomes greater, stronger. There is no limitation to the expansion. You say you have gone to the moon in your lifetime. A thousand years from now you will be traveling to other galaxies. It all has to do with progress, evolutionary studies and the progress of the universe.[5]

maybe could we be clones, designed from another planet?

Aenka spoke simply of an individual soul's part in progressive evolution. "You are an entity and part of your Heavenly Father. From the Source you are born and to the Source you will return. Your physical body is only a vehicle for the first step of your own evolution."

THE SPIRITUAL JOURNEY

After birth from the Source, all of us as souls/entities have much to experience and learn, many challenges to meet, before we merge back and add our tiny unique bit to an expanding God and an evolving universe. This section highlights in overview fashion the progressive evolutionary journey we all share. While all souls must go through the same developmental levels, there is enormous individuality and uniqueness in the process and the end result. In our individual growth patterns, by plan and by accident, much variation occurs in the path we take and the duration of our stay on any one level or step.

Upon birth from the Source we enter the unobstructed. While there we do not carry the shape of a physical body but exist as patterns of spiritual energy. Our spiritual essence in the unobstructed is "pure spiritual energy, facets of the Source of All Divinity." The entities find it difficult to describe this state of existence in physical terms and words familiar to us. They speak of brilliant patterns of color, each charged with spiritual and psychic energy, roughly comparable in the obstructed to the beauty and uniqueness of snowflakes. In the unobstructed universe time and space do not exist in the way that we know them, and while there we have extreme awareness of many aspects of both the unobstructed and obstructed universes. We communicate with other entities by what we in the physical might call thought transference, which Mario describes as simply "awareness."

After birth from the Source, our first task in the unobstructed is to make some early choices. We choose what aspects of physical life we want to challenge in our first physical incarnation, the general goal being to acquire as many of the necessary experiences as possible. We also begin to consider and possibly choose one of three major areas of study that will be a special focus for us throughout our physical lives. These three major areas, as categorized by man, are generally art, science, and religion. According to the entities, all human endeavor can be viewed as falling into one or another or a combination of these somewhat arbitrary categories.

The planning of our first physical life is based on many factors; and with the expanded awareness we have while in the unobstructed, we do our best to plot our individual destiny in the physical. As entities in the unobstructed, we confer with our soulmates and other entities in setting up possible influences that those remaining in the unobstructed might bring to bear while we are in the body. Such influences assist us in our attempt to complete our chosen destiny for that time period. We literally choose our parents-to-be, as well as the part of the planet where we are to have our first physical incarnation.

Despite this planning process, and even though we are aware of many factors, it is impossible to predict for our physical future exactly how these factors may change when they interact with other forces. The most we can do is compute probabilities concerning possible future events, occurrences, influences. All of this planning is referred to as the "government of life," which might be simply described as all of the guidance forces and factors that we put into motion before we incarnate into a physical body.

When we have chosen the experiences we wish to challenge in our first physical lifetime, computed the probabilities, and designed our plan of influence as well as we can, we as souls then enter a physical body. Our soul begins to enter the body of an infant at about the time the infant takes the first breath on its own. Prior to this time we simply monitor the development of the physical fetus. When we enter the body we go through a process of solidifying in the body, and it may be said in a sense that our soul takes possession of that body. This solidifying process does not relate to the erroneous concept of possession by evil spirits or demons, but to the sense of a constructively motivated soul using the body as a vehicle to gather positive physical experiences. From the time of solidification until the body dies, our spiritual aspect is inextricably intertwined with our physical, emotional, and intellectual aspects.

Once fully stabilized in the infant's body, we rather quickly lose conscious awareness of our true spiritual nature and the knowledge available to us while we were in the unobstructed. This loss of conscious awareness of our soul and its knowledge is referred to by the entities as "the curtain being drawn" and is part of the Source's design to offer even more challenges to the soul's

searching and learning through its physical journey. After this
functional amnesia we are influenced through that physical lifetime primarily by our physical, emotional, intellectual, and spiritual experiences acquired in the body. As Mario put it,

*This is not true either! The spirit always responds
to the awareness function of man — therefore as man
thinks, so he becomes — negative, destructive etc.*

You, the entity or soul within that body, do not initiate
behaviors other than some preconscious maneuvering. It is
not the spirit that manipulates the vehicle. The vehicle has
been designed to function in natural ways to bring forth certain behaviors that will cause or expose one to needed experiences. To have those experiences you must be part of the
physical. But you do not maneuver or manipulate all that
much; primarily you are a guest taking a free ride in the vehicle through life. *The "ride" isn't free if the vehicle
suffers through mis-directed glandular juices!
The medics and psychs as well as lawyers cost!*

While our soul does take the backseat, so to speak, in our
journey through a physical life, it is not quiescent, nor is it totally
unavailable to us. It seeks to influence our physical personality
and behavior in certain directions in order to gather our needed
positive experiences. Our entity within can make contact with the
unobstructed and assist in conveying messages from it to our
physical personality. Some of the avenues utilized are impingement, intuition, dreams, out-of-body experiences (also called
astral travel) and what we in the physical call *psychic experiences.*
"While you cannot manipulate directly, there are degrees of influence that you as the soul or entity in the physical body have
over the body's behavior. The more in tune the physical is with
the preconscious, the more apt it is to live in harmony." The factors of the curtain being drawn and the lack of ability to directly
manipulate the physical mind and body relate to the necessity for
the government of life. While free choice of physical man's responses to his environment can be significantly influenced by his
own psychological processes, these choices *cannot* be violated by
the entity/soul within. *Ho! Ho! We only know "choice"
when we awaken from patterned thought processes.*

In our first lifetime we live, it is hoped, our threescore and ten. We grow physically, we learn, we work, we marry, we struggle, and through much of adult life we ponder what appears indecipherable—the meaning of life and the nature of God. In our physical life we must endure the hazards of events that can interfere with our now unconscious plan of destiny and the realization of that destiny. Our natural spiritual intuition attempts to guide us in the direction of our chosen destiny and subtly urges us to ways and means of recontacting our spiritual dimension, increasing the awareness of our spiritual essence, and peeking behind the curtain.

Whether through natural deterioration of the body, illness, or accident, the time comes for us to leave our vehicle. The physical body dies; it has served its purpose in providing both a vehicle for, and a challenge to, the tiny part of God that is our soul. After irreversible physical death our soul literally leaves the body and returns to the unobstructed. This transition involves a sequence of experiential processes to assist the soul in reorienting and feeling "at home" once again in the unobstructed.

Back in the unobstructed, after we have made our adjustment to being there, our first task is what the entities call *evaluation*. This is essentially an individual assessment of what we achieved during our first physical life. Which goals did we meet? Which ones did we not reach? What experiences did we gather and assimilate in an accepting manner? What experiences did we miss or distort in an egocentric way? How balanced was our giving and our taking? How freely did we share with others? What did we avoid out of fear? What did we deny out of pride? How successful were we in loving ourselves and others unconditionally? How judgmental were we? How much respect did we show others, how much disrespect or condescension? Did we create anything to the benefit of others individually or collectively? *or benefit SELF?*

The evaluation is thorough and exhaustive. There are *no* judgments of good or bad in this evaluation—it is strictly descriptive and essentially a scorecard, an abacus, a logbook of work completed and of work yet to be completed. The evaluation results in a simple registration of this information, and then we turn our attention to tasks at hand in the unobstructed.

Now back in our original energy form, we extend our awareness and allow much information to register. We greet and communicate with other entities. If our soulmates are in the unobstructed, we communicate with them and share information. After a familiarization period we become even more firmly and fully at home, and we begin our work there.

The type of work we do in the unobstructed varies. There is much study of the physical energies of the universe, of the universal laws that determine the function of those energies, and of the many universal laws that the Source designed to guide the activities of entities in and out of the physical body. There are moments of communication/communion with the Source that nourish and replenish our energy.

One function available in the unobstructed is to serve as what is commonly called a *spirit guide* to those in the body, becoming involved to a large or small degree with the government-of-life plans for a number of other entities. In this capacity we attempt to impinge on entities in the physical body in an effort to nudge or urge them to choose certain directions. However, in the unobstructed we have definite limits on how much we can influence those in the body, for they must face their challenges primarily on their own. Free choice of a physical personality cannot be violated. As spirit guides we cannot act as puppeteers. The most we can do is act as the gentlest of guides, although occasionally a more drastic influence is allowed.

After we do all these things in the unobstructed for a period of time determined by our own choice, based on our involvement with other entities and our own unique destiny plan, we return to the physical. We *reincarnate*. Very rarely will a soul finish his physical experiences and tasks in one physical lifetime, and should this occur, it is not necessary for that entity to return to a physical body. If we need to reincarnate, we again create a government-of-life plan. We look at what we still need to experience, compute various possibilities and probabilities of influences of the physical structures, and devise our plans with the complicity of other entities. We once more choose a set of parents and, as the fetus is to be born, we are off on another adventure into the physical.

The entities consistently teach that reincarnation is one of the cornerstones of the Source's fail-safe plan. It ensures that we shall have as many opportunities as we need to gather all our experiences in the physical. Regardless of the extent to which we miss or invalidate experiences of learning in any one lifetime, there will be other opportunities. The entities also emphasize that concerning unfulfilled aspects of destiny or the mistakes we make, there is absolutely no sin or guilt attached. We literally have all the time we need to complete our learnings.[6]

The popular concept of karma, applied as it often is to a punitive/rewarding influence over lifetimes, is erroneous. The entities teach that karma is nothing more than natural consequences during a lifetime—not a punishment in a later life for previous transgressions, nor bonus points for past achievements. We are not born into a station in life depending on the quality of our previous physical life. We choose each lifetime on the basis of what we are challenging that particular time around.

Of the many people who think of karma as a punitive force, some will be relieved and others will be resentful of this point of view. Could it be that such resentment is at least partially based on the taking away of an easy answer to one's problems in living during this particular lifetime? If one is a compulsive drinker or has difficulty holding jobs, it is a relatively safe and easy explanation to accept the idea that one is "paying for" some transgression in a previous life. Another part of such resentment may be related to a feeling of superficial superiority; thus one deserves a better life next time around as a reward for work well done or misfortune stoically endured.

The entities describe seven steps in our individual evolutionary progression. Our work and study in physical incarnations is Step

One of this process. The remaining six we work on while in the unobstructed universe. The alternating pattern of activity periods in the obstructed and unobstructed universes is also a part of the Source's fail-safe design. Even though we may require hundreds of physical incarnations to complete our learning in Step One, we can be progressing through Steps Two to Five in the alternate activity periods in the unobstructed. Thus, while a soul in the body is always working on Step One, during the previous period in the unobstructed it could have been studying and functioning anywhere from Steps Two through Five.

The entities state, however, that we cannot go beyond Step Five in the unobstructed until we complete Step One in the physical. After we complete Steps Six and Seven, we merge with the Source. Our work in the obstructed and unobstructed is complete, and we carry home with us the fruits of our labors to add to the incredible complexity of God.

The steps or levels of spiritual evolution that we all must experience in no way correlate to what many students of spirituality refer to as *higher* or *lower spirits, good* or *evil spirits, ascended masters*, and the like. All entities in the unobstructed are described as equal in their access to knowledge and solely positive in their motivation. The entities are emphatic that there is no negative, evil, or destructive energy originating from the unobstructed or the Source. Evil is described as a product of man, not of God or spirit.[7] Satan and hell do not exist in any reality. They are man-made constructs created for the purpose of manipulating people.

Some readers may be dismayed to hear that the entities discourage an excessive focus on some of the more esoteric aspects of spirituality while we are physically incarnated. They emphasize that the reason we incarnate is to acquire experiences we can have only while in a body. To spend too much time seeking escape from the challenges of physical life with its many frustrations will ultimately slow down our spiritual progression.

In general, the entities encourage what they consider a more constructive use of spirituality along the lines of learning how to live a more balanced and rhythmic life in our physical and emotional relationships, striving to master the experience of unconditional love. Man can constructively use, or destructively misuse, the broader concepts and simple daily life experiences of spirituality as well as more dramatic spiritual or psychic experiences. Such choices are part of our free will.

In response to a question about appropriate and inappropriate spiritual emphasis in the physical, with particular reference to the teaching that when we are in the body Step One is the only step we can work on, Aenka stated:

> Yes, that is very difficult to believe and contrary to most if not all of your religious understandings. Many strive to reach or rise above the physical, trying to gain some tremendous enlightenment or spiritual growth. That is not the procedure you must take. The physical is the first step of spiritual evolution and one of the most difficult to master. What you can do is use the Facet of Divinity or that spiritual part of you to open a channel of spirituality, to be in contact with this facet of your personality so it can be beneficial for you; to understand how to approach the physical in a more humble manner.

While the entities consistently emphasize that Step One is one of the most difficult levels to complete, they insist that it is possible to achieve the main goal of living in the physical. This they call *rhythmic living*. Rhythmic living refers to an integrated balance as we interact with other people and our environment physically, emotionally, and intellectually. In working towards this goal, a person becomes gradually more aware of his or her spiritual aspect. This increasing awareness adds a quality of humility to the goal of unconditional love.

[handwritten margin notes:]

"Rhythmic living" or integration is experienced only when one makes a complete turn-about in their life from automatic reactions, responses and judgments. This requires conscious work not belief or philosophy.

personality is that programmed or conditioned from birth, aspect of man. The reality of man has no self — Inv. should

no insights. It is awareness of conditions that evolve into the moment to moment discernment — anger, guilt, fear — into humility.

What is "unconditional love" to you? To me, it is knowing that whatever is happening in your awareness — even if it is totally conditioned — is right, proper and justified for you. Understanding without judgment is Agapé or love.

The first level is the totality of physical experience. All of your physical experiences must be accounted for in a rhythmic nature. If one would become so acquainted with the physical body to know all of its natural hungers—physical, emotional, intellectual, and psychological hungers—they would recognize there are rhythmic patterns designed for these functions. The experience of rhythm is definitely a beautiful thing.

Early spiritual man is said to have lived in a much more natural and rhythmic manner than his more recent counterparts have for the last many thousands of years. The quality of primitive life was more simple on an individual basis and more balanced in the interactional social context. There was less greed, less competitiveness, more respect for one another, more sharing and caring, and more awareness of our spiritual nature. A second volume, now in progress, will describe how this natural rhythm was distorted (or, as the entities say, "broken") and how man has become increasingly influenced by fear, guilt, and greed. Man's historical detour from natural rhythmic living makes the successful completion of Step One even more challenging for contemporary incarnated souls. As Aenka put it,

Because of the broken rhythm it is necessary that reincarnation be of most importance. This is because you cannot always experience opposites or complementary experiences in any one lifetime; for example, positive aggression and its opposite, positive submission. *Ho, ho, ho!*

Even though collective man is said to have detoured considerably, the entities are eternally optimistic both of his individual experience as a Facet of Divinity and of his collective future on earth.

It is possible and hopeful in the years to come that the beginning, or the primitive beginning, of the understanding and the experience of rhythmic living will become so well known to human beings they can establish everything in patterns in a relatively short period of time. One lifetime is more than enough time to gain all experiences in a natural state for which they were intended. If they are exaggerated in any significant form we must come back and relive it.

+ surely us.

If this broad view of emergence, work and study, and eventual return to God sounds a bit mechanical, it is due to the authors' ineptitude with words. The journey is anything but mechanical. It is filled with love, joy, pain, exasperation, despair, and moments of exhilaration. And while the challenges and obstacles we are to face and surmount are formidable, the result is inevitable: we do return to God. The Source's fail-safe design guarantees this return. *and we can do it and real-ize it here and now!*

Concerning the ultimate experience of reunion with the Source, Mario said:

There is great celebration, and the experience is maximum. It is the greatest thing one can experience. There is no other thing that can be experienced that gives you more pleasure. If you could think in terms of multiplying some physical pleasures a million times, that would be the delight you experience when you enter or merge with the Source of divinity. The height of physical pleasure that the body can experience is physical orgasm, or the completion of a challenging task— the ecstasy or the sheer emotional and psychological pleasure. It is very difficult to describe the spiritual reunion in a manner that a physical mind can comprehend. I do not say this to intimidate you, or to challenge your capabilities. If one had ever experienced astral travel, out-of-body experience, it would be equivalent to the grandeur the body

only if he went in pain or psychologically ill?

we never leave this source—we only think it with conditions, although negativity and immaturity eclipse our infinity

A physical mind? I should wonder if a "physical mind" would even consider "a return to God." Physicalness is not eternal.

feels when you have been out of your body and you are reentering. Tremendous . . . you cannot express it . . . ecstasy? Well, what else could you call it? Exhilaration, yes. I believe there is no amount of flashing lights or experiences that one could have in the physical that could explain the Mardi Gras of entering the Source of Divinity.

CHAPTER TWO

The Unobstructed Universe

We can't see ~~or touch~~ atoms; they are not a perceivable part of our world. Yet much of physics is based on the existence of atoms. We can't le without touching atoms. —Marci McCormick!

—Heinz Pagels

What is it like in the unobstructed universe? In what form do we exist there? How do we function, communicate? What do we work on in the six steps of evolutionary growth there? These questions are provocative and meaningful, and they are addressed in this chapter; but please bear in mind that physical life is Step One of spiritual growth. To avoid the challenges of the physical by escaping into totally esoteric spiritual experiences is simply a detour.

You do not work on Steps Two through Seven while you are on Step One. You can only work on those levels between physical incarnations when you are in the unobstructed. When you are in a physical body you work with Step One. What you can do while in the physical is use that spiritual part of you to open your channel of spirituality. This can be beneficial to you and help you understand how to approach

19

the physical in a more harmonious manner. Unfortunately, in many cases the mind tries to rise above and reject the physical procedures. With such attempts, it is understandable why one must return so many times, because little is accomplished while in the physical body.

Birth from the Source

As entities we are born from the Source directly into the unobstructed as unique patterns of pure spiritual energy.

The entity comes from that great Source as though the Source had given birth. An entity—or soul—is a facet that is directed to a mission and allowed to break away from the Source. This fragment may be said to be born from the belly of the body of the Source and will remain separate until it completes its destiny. Every ten cycles of your earth around your sun, those entities that are ready will merge with the Source to become part of It again. You need not concern yourself with questions such as adequate numbers of entities for bodies; this is not a meaningful issue.

What would these energy patterns/entities look like if we saw them with physical eyes?[1] How do they communicate?

How can I describe the beauty? They are multifaceted, with indescribable colors of the entire spectrum far beyond physical limits. The colors are in patterns, each unique in configuration. The intensity is great, more than, for example, your psychedelic or strobe lights. Size varies from about the size of a snowflake to twelve of your inches, somewhat spherical in shape, like a starburst. You do not use language, you are simply aware of frequencies and patterns of different energies in both the obstructed and the unobstructed universes. It is very difficult to explain this awareness, what it is like. It would be more in the form of sensory awareness than thinking, compared to the physical. But how do you compare? For we have no physical body and thus no physical senses. Think of it as thought pictures with the equivalent of sensory awareness—no words. We expand and contract in communication and responsiveness. When we are involved in things of excitement and ecstasy, we expand. Response is thus indicated in one manner by the behavior of an energy pattern. You might compare this responsiveness to when you are responding emotionally to external stimulation in the physical. You may feel tantalized or elated, but you have a variation of emotional responses, and these are expressed in your body. So if you were communicating to me, as spirit, my energy pattern would respond according to how I was affected or influenced by your communication. When I am not materialized, that is when I am in my current natural state as an energy pattern, I "view" your complete energy pattern. I am aware of your back as well as your front at the same time. Your sight is a physical phenomenon, you see, and is thus obstructed by matter. My awareness is not restricted by matter.

As souls, we are never born alone, and those entities created with us are referred to as soulmates.

Soulmates . . . a beautiful arrangement which the Source developed from the very beginning, the better to bear the journey from the Source to the Source. It makes the journey interesting that you have a mate, and are interdependent. Entities are born from the Source in pairs, never singly. Sometimes, more often than you may imagine, three entities are born. Occasionally five are born together, but never four. There can be any configuration regarding sexual identity but each sex is always represented. It may be one male, two female. With five it could be one female and four males.

Having one or more soulmates ensures that we do not make our total spiritual journey through the levels alone. Soulmates are of much importance and value to one another in several ways both in the obstructed and unobstructed universes. Ultimately the plan of having soulmates ensures that we shall learn interdependence in addition to independence.

The importance of sharing experiences in the physical with a soulmate is underscored by the following statement:

In the design of spiritual energy all things must be given motion and direction and be significant in experience. Soulmates were designed under the universal law for a specific purpose: total experience in the physical having to do with individual and joint destiny. Had this not been incorporated into the natural processes and experiences, then the species would not be so apt to take seriously or gain any joint destiny commitment that could really be appreciated. You must live at least one positive physical life with your soulmate. If you are incarnated during the same time frame, there will be an unconscious spiritual yearning to be with and to experience interdependence. It is a drive that pulls you spiritually to seek out, a hunger to find and be committed to. Both individual and joint destiny must be experienced, so that you will know and understand interdependence.

Soulmates in the unobstructed plan physical lives together in pursuing their joint destiny plans.

If you have not lived a physical life together, your soulmate and you shall seek out a possible arrangement and program the government of life to bring you together. The entities will seek each other out in a physical life and fall in love [not necessarily romantic love]. The government of life shall do whatever possible to draw you together, anything short of violating a universal law.

The importance of the bond between soulmates is so great that, should entities be ready to merge with the Source while their soulmates are not, "they shall wait for each other. They cannot merge with the Source until they both or all are ready."

While shared experiences with one's soulmates are necessary and important for all souls, this does not obviate the individual destiny of each individual soul. Soulmates are to share with, and not to be used to avoid one's unique individual destiny.

Once born into the unobstructed, "entities are on their own to choose when and where they start their journey." During our first experience in the unobstructed, we devote much time to making some early choices regarding our first physical incarnation. "The entity must program and decide his destiny, and look for a physical body." We do not actually begin unobstructed studies per se in Step Two until after our first life in the physical body.

> When you start your second level there is not enough "time lapse" between when you are born from the Source until you accept your physical body. There is no time to work on the level other than decisions regarding your first physical life.

One of our early choices focuses on what experiences in the physical we will seek to challenge and, it is hoped, obtain during our first incarnation. Included in these are physical, emotional, intellectual, and spiritual experiences that all of us must gather, plus the choice of a major field of study. "You choose a major thrust in life, whatever area you wanted to master. Prior to your birth you would program the government of life. Most likely your choice would be the category that you would eventually find yourself involved with." While we each choose a major focus, we must also gain a working knowledge of all three general areas. Typically, we emphasize one of the areas as more or less a major interest throughout all our physical lifetimes.

Another early choice during our neonatal period in the unobstructed is that of parents for our first incarnation. While in the unobstructed, we can literally observe, monitor, and have considerable awareness of many reality factors in the physical world.

"You are in constant observation. Your choices of parents are based on what your planned needs are. You select the environment, the culture, and the parents that offer you the potential of the greatest challenge for experiences you need."

Mario startled us when he said that one of the reasons for our choice of parents was "because you have evaluated their pathology and what they are apt to do to influence you." He went on to explain that by *pathology* he was referring to personality traits in a descriptive, not a psychiatric or clinical, sense. "What I am making reference to is their personality, the choices they are making, and what they are apt to do with their life, including how they are likely to influence a child."

While choosing with such awareness may seem to drastically improve or even guarantee completely our destiny plans for a lifetime, this is not the case. It is true that we are aware of many factors of the physical world while we are in the unobstructed, but these factors are not static or unchangeable. We cannot predict the future with any certainty because there are simply too many variables, each of which is in an evolving or changing process of its own. The most we can do is compute probabilities regarding the future.

There are also unpredictable events in the lives of individuals and cultures that are the result of sheer accident, as well as collective and individual changes. All of these unknown factors constitute what the entities call the "gamble of life." Such uncertainties are said to be an intentional aspect of the Source's design for evolutionary changes, to offer greater challenge and to ensure opportunity for a wide variety of learning experiences.

The gamble of life applies to our choice of parents in that regardless of how they are personally functioning at the time of the birth of a child, their parenting behavior may change significantly during the formative years of the child. As Mario describes it, the best we can do in the unobstructed is to choose parents "according to where they are psychologically when you accept the body. But they could change drastically after the child is born and you have accepted the body. A year later they could become monsters, and you would have an entirely different experience than you had calculated."

Contact between Entities and the Source

While in the unobstrcted, *all* entities experience moments of direct contact with the Source. Mario describes the experience of such contact in glowing and expressive terms: "It is like a nurturing. It enhances, it revitalizes, it makes you feel—if there could be for us in the unobstructed an emotional attachment or the equivalent—if there were a translation to it—it would be like falling in love every second."

According to Mario, either the Source or an entity can initiate this contact. However, at the initiative of the entity, "it is just as difficult for me to contact the Source as it is for you to contact us in the unobstructed." Regardless of the frequency of such contacts, "it is rare that I would have that privilege or that need; of course, you must realize it is never as much as I might like it to be, because of the experience and what it does to your energy." While the frequency of these contacts for any one entity may be relatively rare, "if you are talking about trillions of entities, then it is common, there is always someone doing it."

The experiences of direct contact between entities in the unobstructed and the Source serve several purposes.[2] In addition to being a nurturing and energizing experience for the entity, the Source makes contact "to monitor and to determine whether or not the energies are functioning in an order that they were designed to function, to evaluate progress and to ensure continuity."

The more usual contact and relationship between entities in the unobstructed and the Source is in a very real sense similar to the potential contact and relationship that we in the physical have with entities in the unobstructed—that is, an ongoing interaction of subtle influences with moments of peak experiences. Entities in the unobstructed are much more aware of this type of contact and influence than are we in the obstructed, as they have no physical personality to interfere and through which communications must filter.

How does time work in the unobstructed?

It does not, at least not as you know it. We are not governed by time, we are governed by experience. We are well aware of time—past, present, and future—but that is mostly relative to how you measure time. We are aware that it has been twelve or so of your years since we first had an opportunity to communicate with you in a materialized form. But we do not think of it or respond to it as you do, as having been twelve years. We respond to it as an experience, whether it was a hundred years or fifteen minutes.

Can we go back in time as we measure it in either the obstructed or unobstructed universe? "No, you cannot choose a period of evolution and relive it. You can choose to wait a hundred or more of your years before another incarnation, but you cannot turn back what has happened in the physical. You cannot turn back physical time." A comment Mario casually dropped in response to questions about time in the unobstructed will perhaps give you a concept of how they relate to our time: "Well, you could stay on any level for a thousand years, conceivably. But not usually. It depends on how frequently you incarnate."

When it comes to short periods of time, as measured in seconds or minutes compared to years, entities in the unobstructed move with extraordinary rapidity. They have never given us any firm figures in our time framework, but they have made a number of statements suggesting that they can move the equivalent of many millions of miles in a matter of seconds.[3]

You measure time in the smallest amount of light, the speed of light. Some light energies that you have discovered travel faster than others, but all are limited. We can travel much faster than the speed of light. There is little time lapse in our travels, because we are not obstructed by any other energy. We are in charge of our energy patterns to direct it or "beam" it wherever we choose. We desire to be there and we are there, almost instantly. By your reckoning, you would think we are in two places simultaneously but this is not the case. Of course we can have awareness of what occurs elsewhere without actually traveling there, but that is another matter.

STEPS OR LEVELS

The king in a carriage may ride,
And the Beggar may crawl at his side;
But in the general race,
They are traveling at the same pace.
—Edward Fitzgerald

We have already mentioned that there are no hierarchies of entities in the unobstructed, no higher or lower spirits, no superior or inferior beings. Yet the entities speak of "steps" or levels of spiritual progression. Does this not imply at least a minimum of time for study and the acquisition of knowledge as we move through the levels or steps? The entities say no and resolve this apparent paradox by explaining their context concerning measurement of knowledge as related to their experience of time. All entities in the unobstructed are said to have access to all recorded knowledge. Thus no one entity may be said to be more knowledgeable than another. Progression through the unobstructed steps does not depend on knowledge but rather on gathering *experiences* in a way similar to that encountered in physical life.

Growth is experience, not necessarily knowledge. Knowledge is no more or less accessible to any one entity than it is to any other. Growth and progress is thus related to experience and comprehension, not intellectual knowledge alone. You can know something, be very familiar with it in theory or knowledge, but not have experienced it. The only differences between entities on different steps or levels are in what they are acquiring by experiencing different things. If I went to Jupiter and told you everything I had experienced, you would have that knowledge would you not? But it would not have been your experience. I cannot experience your required experience. Experience cannot be communicated to another. Knowledge can, facts. But you cannot communicate experience. If you had to walk a mile, and I had walked the same distance, my sharing my experience with you would not fulfill your requirement even if I shared with you the pain or the ecstasy of it. You would have an intellectual awareness of what it was like, but you cannot experience something through others.

Although these distinctions made sense to us, we still had difficulty understanding the *effect* of our experiences on evolution and on returning to the Source. How could experience be the crucial factor in spiritual growth or the measurement of time passage? Surely an entity on Step Five has completed more experiences than an entity on Step Three? Does this not make him more knowledgeable in some way, "higher," than an entity on Step Three? If not, what is the effect of gaining more experiences in the unobstructed, and what is the difference between an entity on Step Five and one on Step Three?

The only thing more experience does is put you closer to your objective of merging back with the Source. You are wondering about the influence that it has on the energy pattern? On the entity? I must be lost for words. Even though we have different personalities and vibrations of our energy . . . it appears that there are no descriptions of it in your words because there is no hierarchy, there is no competition, there are no levels of superiority in the unobstructed. So therefore, how does it influence you or affect one? It puts one closer to finishing. It does not make you anything. It simply puts you closer to finishing. Bear in mind, all knowledge is available to all entities. It is difficult, I am sure, to conceive that levels of intelligence are equally distributed. Each one of us [in the unobstructed] has a different perspective, but those perspectives must conform to the universal law whereby there is no competition. Therefore superiority, or levels of such, do not exist.

Prompted by some psychic and spiritual writings that speak of levels of souls in the spiritual world, and in reference to what man on earth does with feelings of superiority and inferiority, we asked for some elaboration regarding these issues. Aenka responded that while there is no such thing as hierarchical levels in the unobstructed, there are a variety of "working" organizational groups of entities. Any one entity may be a coordinator of one particular group and a working member of another. In any particular configuration, each entity would have his own function.

There are, for example, many loosely organized groups in the unobstructed that focus on impingement to those of us in the physical, "groups of entities that support various organized thought patterns beneficial to individuals' progressive development." Aenka used his own involvement with our darkroom group, of which he serves as coordinator for other entities interested in the participants, as an example of such a group.

Although we are delegated to work in the field of psychological development, you must remember that whatever subject an entity chooses, all impingement must be aimed at the objective—which is harmony. Entities in the unobstructed would classify which interests they would support, their impingement hopefully encouraging you to develop in one of the areas of your choosing.

Mario referred to another organized working group in the unobstructed in referring to himself and Aenka as being involved with what they call the K Plan.

The entity K has elected as a focus of his spiritual destiny the supervision of a coordinated effort in the unobstructed regarding psychological movement and development on earth. This effort is referred to by the entities as a "revolution against negativity" and has as its goal the return of man to natural rhythmic living; to bring man back to the rhythmic personality and awareness of the potential for unconditional love, and that within each person is the awakening of their true spirituality.

In the unobstructed we follow a major area of study, but this does not mean that we limit our studies or involvement to the major; we merely emphasize that area. Indeed, it is often possible for a number of entities with different interests to join together in a group effort, each contributing his own perspective and all benefiting in unique ways. For example, the entire K Plan takes in all three categories of art, science, and religion.

In the working groups, is all peaches and cream? Are there never disagreements as to priorities and individual contributions as exist in the obstructed? It appears that while indeed there may at times be disagreement regarding choices, any possible ongoing conflict between entities is impossible.

We can feel very deeply for a person in the sense of understanding, but we have no feelings as you know them. We do not argue. We have no ego to offend. When you have no fear or guilt, what is there to offend? We cannot do things that would violate rhythmic patterns. We consider the welfare of each individual. It is a matter of discussion for entities as to which choice would likely be the more constructive, which direction would be the more positive. When a decision is made, it is never accepted with reluctance. It is moved toward with positive submission and total acceptance.

GOVERNMENT OF LIFE

Once we have made our choices regarding what we want to challenge in our first incarnation, selected a fetus and parents, and made any plans we wish with our soulmates, we turn our attention to planning what is called our government-of-life system. "When you have determined those things you need to experience, then you set forth and design your program, your needs, into the government of life." The phenomenon and functioning of the government of life is, for the authors, a fascinating process. Essentially what we do in programming our government-of-life plan is to store information concerning our decisions in what is referred to as the "archives."

Mario and Aenka describe these archives as comparable to a library. Our government-of-life plan is literally recorded, and the information is obtainable by any entity who desires it. Thus do our guides, when we are incarnated, have reference by which to assist us. The government-of-life archives are part of, and similar to, the more general and vast archives of knowledge of which many people have spoken. The structure and function of the government-of-life archives may be best explained by sharing what we have been told of the more general archives of knowledge.

ARCHIVES OF KNOWLEDGE

Even the hairs of your head are all numbered.
—Matthew 10:30*

The archives of knowledge (or Akashic Records) is a repository of information that is very much a reality, not merely a concept.

*All Bible quotations are taken from the Lamsa translation of the Holy Bible.

The archives of knowledge is a place where all things are recorded. It is equivalent to you seeing books on your library shelves and identifying them.

Mario attempted to help us visualize such a place within our concept of three-dimensional thinking.

I can only say that it looks like the archives of knowledge. You could not see it with your physical eyes, but we are aware of those types of energies stored as information of which it consists. It is a space and an energy very obvious to those of us in the unobstructed. It is there. It would be like going to your library. Do you have a library card? I have a key to our library. If we choose, we can visit and study. Each entity has potential total awareness, meaning all knowledge is available to each of us.

Information in the archives of knowledge is said to have been recorded there "from the beginning of creation."

In response to further questions in our attempts to physically visualize how information could be stored in a (to us) nonphysical place, Mario used an analogy to a computer.

Can you see the energy patterns stored as information in the computer or on the computer tape? No, but it is there nonetheless. In a similar way we are aware of energy spaces in this area of knowledge. We perceive or identify the energy recorded there. Any individual bit of information is identified, in a sense, with a name on it. It is difficult to be literal in the translation. Can you tell the difference between cool air and warm air? How do you know whether it is cool or warm? Yes, you feel the difference through your sensory apparatus, you have identified the energy.

Mario went on to say that such a simple differentiation, magnified a thousand or a million times, might help us understand how entities locate or become aware of information bits in the archives.

Every behavior, every response from you, every reaction is
recorded within the archives of knowledge.[4]

The entities say these sweeping statements are not generalizations,
but fact. According to them, the entire history of each entity ac-
crues in a progressive fashion in his "cubicle." This information
is public knowledge in the sense that any other entity has access to
it should the need arise. In that part of the archives of knowledge
relative to government-of-life plans, entities who need information about someone incarnated "can check the archives appropriate to them. It would be in their cubicle, so to speak. If by
chance the needed information is not there, they could review the
experience of another entity." In the case of needing information
about discarnate entities, "they could also of course communicate
directly with that entity for more information."

There is not one but rather many archives of knowledge in the
unobstructed.

In each galaxy that supports life, entities have their own archives of knowledge. You can study and learn about them,
and you must, before you graduate. Only a small part of the
knowledge stored in those archives is applicable when you are
working as guides with individuals in this physical galaxy.
But entities must learn it even though we might never have
the pleasure or privilege of working with those universal laws
that govern the behavior of the physical in other galaxies.

SPIRIT GUIDES

*For he shall give his angels charge over you to keep you in all
your ways.*

—Psalms 91:6

Once we record our government-of-life plan and make ready to
enter an infant body for our first life in the physical, a number of
other entities still in the unobstructed make a commitment to

serve as helpers or guides to us during that physical incarnation. One entity serves as what is called a *main guide*, others as *secondary* or *supportive guides*. The entities who elect to serve as guides will attempt to influence us throughout our physical life according to our government-of-life plan. One way they do so is by impingement—a psychic nudge to pay attention to certain thoughts, feelings, urges, dreams, wishes, hunches, or aspects of the environment. While at times, in conjunction with other guides, they may manipulate physical forces in our interest, they *cannot* violate any laws of physical energy or free choice by the individual they are influencing. A concrete example of one way guides influence us in relation to the government of life and soulmates was given by Aenka and may prove illustrative. How do soulmates manage to get together in a physical life?

Say that you have not succeeded in a positive relationship in the physical with your soulmate. You are in the unobstructed and your soulmate has just made a choice to incarnate in New York. The two of you need a positive experience in a physical life. You would program into the government of life to be maneuvered into a relationship with your soulmate. You choose a family, parents, in Montreal. Now when you are born into the body you have total amnesia, but as your physical body matures and you grow into adulthood, or possibly before adulthood, your guide—or the government of life—would attempt to maneuver you by impingement. This would be in such a way that it would hopefully influence you, but it would never be in a way that would violate your free choice. You would feel an urge, subtly, to move to New York. Or she would feel an urge to move to Canada.

Further descriptions of the functions of spirit guides will be given in this chapter when Step Four of evolutionary progression is discussed.

STEP ONE—FIRST INCARNATION

When I was born, I drew in the common air, and fell upon the earth.

—Apocrypha, Wisdom of Solomon 7:3

Upon entering an infant body, we begin our first experiences in the physical. The entrance is somewhat gradual as the soul/entity needs a certain amount of time to solidify and become "one with" the body. After we are solidified in the body, the curtain is drawn.

> You have no awareness of what has taken place. Your mind must develop into spiritual awareness through natural physical progression in order to bring these facts to consciousness. If an individual is allowed to develop physically and psychologically in a rhythmic manner, he or she shall upon entering young adulthood have their spiritual facet begin to blossom.

In the sense that a soul actually enters a body and uses it as a vehicle for its experiences, the entities speak of a soul as "possessing" a body. However, it sould be made clear that they are not speaking of control of the body such as is found in popular fiction, where beings are said to be "possessed by an evil spirit" or made to do things "against their will." Entities speak of possession *only* in the sense of a positive spark of God literally using the human body as a vehicle through which to gather experiences. The entity within can attempt to nudge and influence in positive spiritual directions, but it is a universal law that they absolutely cannot interfere with the individual's freedom of choice.

Physical life is the most challenging and difficult step of all, and the entities intimate that most of us need many lifetimes to complete the experiences in this step of growth. However, it is *possible* in one lifetime. "If he gains all of his positive experiences in one lifetime, there would be no need to return, and he would not choose to have another physical life. He would complete Step Two and continue to design and evaluate his future destiny, then experience it in the unobstructed.'' While the entities say that this is possible, they suggest that at the present time it is not very likely. They explain the difficulty in part by referring to how far away from rhythmic living man has moved. The more distorted our natural behaviors and progressions are, the more difficult it is to be in tune with what one needs to accomplish in a spiritual sense.

In far distant times, when man was more aware of his spiritual connection, more entities completed their needed experiences in one lifetime. The shortest time given for any one entity to complete his learning in one lifetime was thirty-three years. The progression of an incarnated entity through a physical life, the death process, and the transition back to the unobstructed will be considered in chapter 6. We will also speak of reincarnation and impingement from the unobstructed as experienced from the physical point of view. This chapter continues to focus on the unobstructed.

First Evaluation

If I have done well, and as is fitting . . . it is that which I desired; but if slenderly and meanly, it is that which I could attain unto.
—Apocrypha, 2 Maccabees 15:38

After our first physical life, we return to the unobstructed. One of the first functions we conduct upon return is what the entities call "evaluation." An evaluation is primarily a tallying up of experiences in the previous physical life. How much did we achieve, what did we miss, where did we make mistakes in what we hoped to gain?

Your evaluation is a record of your behavior, your rhythmic behavior. For example, if in one of your lives you experienced positive aggression and its opposite—positive submission—that is noted in your evaluation and goes into the archives of knowledge.

Evaluation is thus essentially a process of logging achieved experiences and mistakes or failures in a tally sheet. However, unlike the single-chance Judgment Day described by some Christian religions, we have as many opportunities in the physical as we need to complete our positive experiences. These experiences are accumulated over many lifetimes, and we do not need to repeat those that are adequately gained. Those not yet acquired go into government-of-life plans relevant to subsequent incarnations.

It is important to understand at least two aspects of the evaluation process. (1) We conduct our own evaluation based on our unique destiny plan; no one evaluates our behavior except ourselves. We are our own assessor—and it is impossible to be dishonest in this task. (2) The evaluation is strictly descriptive. There are no value judgments, no pats on the back, no guilt, no sin, no ego trips.

REINCARNATION

Plato affirmed that the soul was immortal and clothed in many bodies successively.
—Diogenes Laertius, from Plato 40

The purpose of reincarnation into the physical is quite simply to allow ample opportunity "to gain all experiences necessary, for they must be shared or experienced in a natural state which was intended. If they are distorted in any form, you must come back and relive them."[5] Aenka described this needed repetition by making an analogy to attending a university.

A physical life might be compared to taking a particular class, not receiving a passing grade, and having to take that class over and over until you have a score high enough to say, "I now understand it." After you die and have completed your evaluation, you determine if it is necessary to have another physical life.[6] If so, then you determine exactly what experience you need to return for. Beginning again on your search for environment you consider parents, culture, and all growth potentials. What you are trying to determine in your assessment and preparation is what will be the effect of the environment on the physical body of the child as it grows. Will it or will it not have the opportunity to develop psychologically or emotionally, enabling the opportunity to experience those things that you need.

Successful completion of a particular aspect of living in the body is defined as gaining experiences of a positive and rhythmic sort to the extent that one then has a working knowledge of that slice of life. Once we master something by this criterion we no longer need to work at repeating that particular experience in the physical. In subsequent incarnations we may or may not repeat these experiences, but we do not *need* to repeat them to ensure our overall spiritual progression. In fact, in a follow-up physical lifetime we may even be out of synch in that particular aspect. Again, this will not interfere with our overall progression if we have already experienced a balance in that aspect and have so logged it in the archives of knowledge.

Hitting the target areas of experience we hope for during a lifetime is apparently not an easy or even simple matter. Although for any single physical life we may design into our government-of-life plans a particular career or work focus that fits our chosen major area of study, there is no guarantee that we will choose it once we are incarnated. Many factors of free choice, parental or other influences, economic necessity, etc., all add to the challenge of hitting this target. "You may work twenty years as a mechanic only to find yourself hobbying or retiring into what the government of life has programmed for you." Indeed, in a very real sense hitting or missing a particular target experience is often not a crucial issue for any one lifetime, for we need to gather a breadth of experience in the physical, and there are many choices. "You may not choose one of your major fields for your study or your livelihood. Usually one will unconsciously choose a category for their livelihood in any particular life that they need the most *experience* in."

Mario used himself in a hypothetical example of how and why a main focus in any one lifetime might not be related specifically to one's overall major area of physical study over many lifetimes.

Say that I have failed miserably in the arts. It is more than likely that I would choose an environment and parents so that my growth process would motivate me to learn about art. I might well hate it. I could be very good in biology or astronomy and it would come easy for me, but I would be motivated by the government of life to study art. So it would appear in my emotional makeup and my intuitive process that my destiny, my real destiny, would be art, when it is no such thing. But you see, you must experience all three areas —art, science, and religion—and have a working knowledge of them before you can graduate from Step Five in the unobstructed.

Mario made it clear we are not to assume that during any one lifetime we focus on, and benefit from, only one primary aspect of gathering experiences. "Just because you are a psychologist does not mean you are not sensitive to art, that you do not have any appreciation of it, or that you are not influenced by it. The artistic part of man is very much a part of the total personality." He also pointed out that in regard to learning more harmonious living in the body, irrespective of our destiny work or major area of study, we are always working to accumulate psychological experiences and emotional balance. "To achieve natural spirituality one must focus a great deal on the psychological imperfections."

While we can accrue many types of positive experiences in a lifetime even though we may miss a particular target, we do in a sense penalize ourselves for botching a clear opportunity. In our subsequent government-of-life plans we purposefully design the challenge to be more difficult the next time around. Aenka spoke of this one night.

It is interesting to note, each time you fail in a physical life to achieve some rhythmic pattern of growth, in a subsequent incarnation you will choose an environment that will make such achievement even more difficult for you. You would think one would choose an environment or a physical body that would be easier, but each failure is compounded to cause the challenge to be even greater. The reason for this is in hopes you will be more aware of the necessity for it. Paradoxically, the more difficult the challenge, the greater the opportunity to experience.

As we shall see in the following section, this aspect of the Source's plan has been mistranslated as either punishment or award.

KARMA

Observe the opportunity.
—Apocrypha, Ecclesiasticus 4:20

The entities did not readily respond to questions regarding past lives and in general deemphasized previous-life experiences in regard to reincarnation. The primary reason for this attitude is that past lives have little relevance to the current physical life. It matters little during this lifetime what we have already finished; the reason we are back in the body is to work on what we have *not* finished.

Most individuals that ask about past lives are almost certain they bring something back with them, an active issue that has direct bearing on some specific aspect of their current life. What we do in response is to play down or minimize this subject and we do it for a reason. What we say, and try to make clear, is that you bring back no negativity with you and no personality traits. Many individuals do not seem to understand this. For example, here is a beautiful person, a very loving and warm feeling individual. Perhaps in your next lifetime you are overly aggressive or hostile. You do not bring a direct influence of your past behavior patterns, and in each life your personality structure may be totally different. In any one life you may choose a physical body that genetically has inherited an arrangement of a feeling extrovert or a thinking extrovert, or a feeling introvert or a thinking introvert. There is no carryover of any personality trait or emotional response pattern. That is what I am trying to explain. You don't bring back with you psychological or emotional characteristics.[7]

Is there, then, nothing that we can bring forward and become aware of, possibly benefit from?

What you do bring back with you is the *essence* of knowledge you have gained in all of your lifetimes; your scientific, artistic, and spiritual experience. You have the essence of the knowledge within you as the entity enters the body, but with the curtain drawn it has to be awakened. I will try to give you a simple descriptive example of such essence. You become an accomplished pianist during a lifetime. In a later physical life you will find playing or learning music relatively easy for you, whereas another physical being finds it difficult to master. In this life if you master mathematics intellectually, in your next life you will have the essence of that knowledge, and math will come easy to you. You will probably need to study a third of someone who had not mastered the science in another life. This is one reason why there is so much jealousy. Someone says, "I have to work twice as hard as you do to learn this." They do not understand that they have it yet to learn, you have already learned it.[8]

Aenka added yet another reason why entities deemphasize previous-life experiences:

> For one other reason we play down previous lives. Your culture, your society, is geared to superiority versus inferiority. So if I told you that you are on the fourth step of spiritual development, you had experienced 370 lives, and your development was that of a genius, you would go out there and not speak to your neighbor because you would feel you are better than him. Admire me, you dumb bastard; I am smarter than you are. It works in the other direction also. When I say fourth step, you feel inferior, you want to be on the fifth because five is higher than four in your mathematical mind and therefore better.

The fact that we make it harder on ourselves in a future incarnation with each failure to acquire a designated experience (not a "miss" but a failed opportunity) in no way suggests a punitive factor or "karmic debt," as many believe. The entities are adamant that we owe no future debts related to behaviors in any given lifetime. A mistake is a mistake, not a sin.

> You have learned to associate karma with some type of punishment or suffering. I say to you, you shall never incarnate to repay a debt for some misdeed previously committed. If this is the karma you are referring to, I shall not speak of it. Until the mind has been washed of this association to karma, I cannot speak intelligently of it.[9]

But surely there must be some spiritual consequence for consciously destructive behavior? For example, would there be no consequence for purposely blinding a person in an act of torture?

> It would be simply that they had removed someone's eye. That is all. A soul would never choose to be born blind to atone for the past. You are not here to repay the debt of a

previous life. You are here to grow and to make this life as comfortable and pleasant for yourself as you can, to gain all of the experiences possible without damaging the growth of yourself or another individual.

Mario and Aenka speak of distorted punitive concepts of karma as similar to distorted concepts of sin and guilt found in many religions. They are emphatic that an accurate concept of karma has nothing to do with sin or guilt.

Karma is nothing more than consequences of your choices, and that is all. Man accepts the responsibility for his choices and behavior. If you make a decision that harms yourself or someone else, you must suffer the consequences. This is simply the law of recompense. There is no punishment or no need to repay ten times, or whatever.

Step Two

Step Two is the beginning level of our unobstructed studies, and we begin these when we are not involved with planning our next physical incarnation or we no longer need to return to the physical. Mario described Step Two as "a very interesting level because it is the beginning of our unobstructed studies and includes some very fascinating experiences."

It is a period of familiarization with the unobstructed, almost like a kindergarten. You begin to study the physical universe: the formulas for all the energies, how they work and how they are organized. As you begin all that research, you not only observe and learn by direct experience but you study in the archives of knowledge. How are the planets in a solar system aligned, how do they relate to each other and influence each other? You do research and make many interesting observations of everything involved in the makeup of planets. For example, you study not only larger organizational systems but how different molecules relate to each other.

Another aspect of Step Two is determining our major field of interest or focus for our unobstructed work. In general, the major areas are similar to those of Step One in the obstructed—art, science, and religion.

You are evaluating and determining the areas of knowledge, the fields of study, and the approaches you are going to take. In the second level you make a choice of what your major field of study will be as you progress through the following levels. Once you have made that decision the choice is irrevocable. It is an important decision and involves considerable deliberation.

In a physical body, with free choice not only allowed but encouraged, we have more latitude and flexibility in our choices than we do as entities in the unobstructed.

You in the obstructed have more right of free choice in changing your mind than do we in the unobstructed. The choice of a major focus of study in the unobstructed is only one example. In your deliberation you must choose carefully, because you only have one chance to make the choice.

Unfortunately, the matter of choosing a major study area for our evolutionary growth in both the obstructed and unobstructed universes is not as simple for the physical mind to conceptualize as it sounds. The complicaton arises due to the interrelationship of the three major areas and to the fact that we must gain at least a working knowledge of all three areas in the unobstructed as well as in the obstructed. Mario attempted to give us a sense of the quality of interrelationships by referring to his own activities:

You cannot have one without the other. It will appear to you at times that I am assisting you with religious processes, but essentially I am talking about history, physical life, and the survival of the species. In a broad sense, I comment upon the biological process of evolution, the importance of natural behaviors in man and basic psychological or emotional responses. If my major were religion, I could still study behaviors. This is so because behaviors are also a ritualistic process, and from one point of view nothing more than ritualistic behaviors performed over and over again. From this point of view behaviors were designed and motivated by awareness of the spiritual connection and its relationship to the continuity of life. Social science can then be a religion or a science, depending on the point of view. In your culture, you tend to view psychology as a science. Other cultures look at it as religion or art. The same with medicine. It is in the field of healing, yet it has a religious or spiritual aspect. The Western intellect has taken this powerful process and put it into physical science because of technologies.

These, then, are the major focal points of study in Step Two: studying the basics of physical energies relative to our galaxy; selecting our major emphasis of study as we move through the unobstructed levels; and of course designing and planning government-of-life plans for our physical incarnations. When we asked about whether entities in Step Two ever function as spirit guides for those in the obstructed, Mario answered, "It is possible."

There have been entities on level two [Step Two] that chose to be someone's guide. It is not a common practice. Most entities on level two interested in this experience would choose to be representative or secondary guides. They would choose individuals to be around whose life they find most interesting, and that entity would work with the person's main guide. The reason for this choice could be a particular incarnated entity's destiny was very fascinating and they would like to be a part of it. So the entity would put their token into the hat, so to speak, to lay claim to be a secondary guide or a representative for that human being. It is not that the experience of being a guide in level two is in any violation of the universal laws. The occurrence would be related to the purpose or the objective of the entity on Step Two.

Just as we conduct an evaluation of our physical life at the end of our transition process back to the unobstructed, we assess our readiness to progress from one level to the next in the unobstructed. Again, the evaluation is a tabulation in the sense of a descriptive assessment. It is not judgmental, and there is no teacher or principal to promote us. We may consult with other entities on readiness, but we promote ourselves.

STEP THREE

Studies in Step Three are primarily an extension of Step Two. In Step Two we begin general studies of the essential microscopic and macroscopic properties of physical energies in the universe: electrical, magnetic, chemical, atomic and subatomic, etc. In Step Three, we begin to study the organizing principles behind these energy laws, particularly the spiritual and evolutionary principles. The objective is to become familiar with some of the subtleties involved in the interaction of physical and spiritual energies with evolutionary processes. While a portion of this learning occurs through direct study, much of it is acquired while serving as "committee" members or organized working groups.

There appear to be at least two types of these committees in Step Three. One type serves a consulting role to entities in Step Two, the other an evaluative function for entities from any level who are seeking an exception to a universal law. In both capacities we work as monitors to other entities, and in so doing, we ourselves learn.

You are asking—if you are potentially all knowledgeable and programmed not to violate universal laws, why do you need someone to monitor you? The answer is, this is a learning process for those in Step Three—to become more acquainted with the vast number of variations in universal laws and the tremendous responsibility involved when it comes to all of the exceptions relating to these laws.

Concerning monitoring of, and consulting with, entities in Step Two,

Mainly, you study and observe the behaviors of entities on Level Two, how they progress, and how they make their decisions based on the universal laws. You are primarily responsible to constantly keep those entities in check, insuring they do not unintentionally violate universal laws in their very busy schedule of study and decision-making.

There are said to be literally thousands of universal laws with which we must become acquainted in the unobstructed, and these laws can become quite intricate. They relate to all aspects of physical, psychic, and spiritual energies and the function of entities. The purpose of gaining a thorough knowledge of the laws and the principles upon which they are based is not only to increase our knowledge and comprehension of their interaction but to learn how to manipulate them for spiritual purposes.

In attempting to explain the necessity for, and function of, committees in evaluating exceptions to universal laws, which apply whether the energies involved be physical, psychic, or spiritual, Mario made several points. Although universal laws are fixed, some exceptions are allowed. Mario refers to "breaking" and "bending" these laws. Regarding the *breaking* of a universal law, this is impossible without approval from either the Source or a committee from Step Three.

We do not make individual choices of that nature. We simply do not. It would be impossible for an entity in the unobstructed to make an exception without approval. It would be in violation of a greater universal law. We cannot permit ourselves to clearly violate: there is no justifiable reason for that. Such would be a negative act, and in the unobstructed you are not permitted.[10]

Regarding *bending* the law, there is a bit of room for self-initiation. Mario added with a chuckle: "We know our limits and we push them. We might push them until they are nearly broken, but we do not surpass them." However, even with bending there are limitations, and then an exception must be sought from a Step Three committee or the Source.

Many universal laws have exceptions. They cannot be violated *except* under certain circumstances. No matter what step you are on, if you are in the process of making a decision or a choice and there was an exception approaching; then a committee of entities on Level Three would assist you in determining whether or not that exception would violate universal laws, your own spiritual progress, or be interfering with free choice more than is allowed regarding those in the physical.

Mario compared the functioning of such organized evaluation groups in Step Three to formal committees or courts in the physical world. "You serve, similar to your committees or courts. It would be somewhat like a panel or a judge, the process of evaluations for exception." What would happen if an entity applying for an exception disagreed with a refusal by the committee?

There would be no thought put into trying to alter the decision, because you could not possibly justify, and there is no need to attempt to justify. There is simply no justification about it.

To disagree in an emotional sense is not a possibility for entities in the unobstructed.

To become angry would be impossible, since in the unobstructed we do not have feelings or emotions as you recognize them. We compute possibilities in our focus on studies and decisions.

Mario limited his examples of possible exceptions to issues involving how much or in what ways a spirit guide might actually interfere on behalf of an incarnated entity. The main laws involved relate to free choice, the government of life, and the gamble of life.

Suppose there was an entity on Level Four who was a main guide for someone. The guide was confronted with what appeared to be a possibility for an exception: in the vast advancement of your nuclear weapons one country was in the process of becoming an aggressor. Universal law says an entity in the unobstructed cannot violate free choice of human beings; they must be permitted their choices. Without applying for an exception, this guide and others could impinge upon individuals and try to encourage or influence them to evaluate a choice they are about to make involving the use of nuclear weapons. Guides can attempt to give them the message that their choice would not be positive, but a guide cannot interfere with action upon this information. Now assume one individual was about to push the red button that would destroy an entire government. It is conceivable in this situation there could be an exception. The guide would take the issue to a committee on Level Three and the committee will evaluate whether or not the guide can create a phenomenon that would keep that individual from pushing the button. It is possible a guide would be allowed to manipulate and interfere with that choice.

If a guide were to be granted an exception in such a situation, there are a number of types of interference possible.

Lives have been saved through exception. Some individual will make a choice and try to perform a physical act only to find themselves spellbound or glued to the floor, so to speak. They try to move but they cannot. They try to speak but their voice will not function. That would be a temporary inter-mitting interference, overriding their choice of action or behavior. But I assure you, as often as there is seemingly such a miracle, it is a rare incident when they do happen.

The authors believe there have been times in our darkroom ses-sions when Mario has *bent* a universal law. For example, he was extremely vague and noncommittal over a period of many months in response to questions about steps in the unobstructed. He would often state after a long pause "I have no permission to speak of that at this time." We assumed he was being monitored, and that the universal law in question was how much information could be shared without interfering with the participants' self-learning needs and their own destiny issues. Finally, he did share a little more. At one point he referred to his being previously close-mouthed. "At that time I did not have permission to share with you about several levels of development." When questioned about his responding somewhat more freely this particular evening, he responded, "I did not and still do not have complete permis-sion, but, you see, I share with you what I can without violation."

STEP FOUR

Here we focus on life in the body, learning as much as we can about all aspects of human life from the unobstructed point of view. We conduct these studies by direct observation of incar-nated entities in physical life and by use of the archives. The most singular aspect of this study in Step Four is accepting the responsibility of serving as a guide to one or more incarnated entities. "You will find most guides are on the fourth level of growth. In other words your guides, whether you have one or thirteen, will probably be on the fourth level."

Aenka offered a general statement concerning the ultimate purpose of spiritual guides as influences on us in the physical: "They are there for one purpose, and this is to offer you the knowledge available to them. They shall not unfairly guide you." The focus of the guides' attention is on attempting to influence and assist incarnated entities in following their government-of-life plans as they pursue their individual destinies.[11] Mario described the responsibility of a guide as considerable and intricate. "A guide must be constantly aware. You have to know what you can and cannot reveal to the physical world."

There are at least three types of spiritual guidance work available to us in the unobstructed. One is functioning as a person's *main guide*. This function carries the most responsibility. When we choose to function as someone's main guide, we remain his spiritual helper throughout his entire physical life. "Your main guide, having chosen you and made a commitment at your physical birth, shall not reincarnate until you leave the physical life. There are exceptions to this, but not likely." A main guide also serves as the coordinator for our secondary guides, entities who wish to assist us and become involved with us to varying degrees at various times in our life.

We can also function as a *secondary guide* to a number of people. In this capacity we function as assistants or consultants to a main guide. As a secondary guide, we cannot attempt to influence an incarnated being without the permission of the person's main guide.

Secondary guides, also referred to as *auxiliary guides*, can be many but have less responsibility towards the individual. They cannot impinge upon you without permission of your main guide. They can also represent you in the unobstructed, or represent your main guide at his request. Some secondary guides choose you immediately as you enter the body, others choose to be around you and assist you years after you are born. *When* they enter into this relationship with you is a matter of need, meaning a need of both discarnate and incarnated entities. They find your life fascinating and choose to be a part of your destiny. What I mean by a part of your destiny is, they choose to be around you and with you, to learn about your behavior and offer insight or impingement. Usually, when you incarnate there are many entities interested in your destiny.

Mario elaborated on the subject of a main guide serving as a coordinator for other guides.

It is like me talking to you now. Anything I say must be approved by your main guide. This is because essentially the physical structure of your nervous system is influenced by its environment. If I come into your environment or impinge on you in any way, some energy will be involved, and that becomes a part of your environment. Any energy form that you experience in your environment influences you in some way. You cannot meet a stranger and say good morning without that brief encounter influencing you in some way. So you see, anything you are exposed to influences you, and your main guide takes the responsibility to see you are influenced in a positive way as much as possible.

It is important to separate this coordinating function of a main guide from what has been called a "gatekeeper" in some spiritual literature. The gatekeeper concept, relating as it does to higher or lower entities, or good and evil spirits, is said to be a distortion.

A third way of serving as a spirit guide is as a *representative* of another guide. In this capacity the entity usually has an interest in being of assistance to a particular person in the physical and, consequently, to their main and secondary guides. He/she would function on an "as needed" basis. One example of serving as a representative involves impingement by a main or secondary guide by means of an attempt at physical materialization or the production of any other type of unique phenomenon usually described by those in the body as visionary. This might occur when the importance of some aspect of spiritual awareness reached a crucial point for an incarnated entity. In order to ensure objectivity for both the discarnate spirit guide and the incarnated entity he is attempting to assist, a main or secondary guide would seek a representative to make the attempted contact. The representative would be the entity attempting to produce the phenomenon.

As can be imagined, there is the possiblity of extraordinary interplay, interaction, and juggling of factors in our function as spirit guides in the unobstructed as we attempt to assist our friends in the obstructed. The main guide, as we have seen, is responsible for functioning as the coordinator of the many possible influences. It is his responsibility to weigh all factors within the context of his charge's government-of-life plan and destiny. Objectivity is very important in functioning as any type of guide, and it is essential for a main guide. For this reason, our soulmates are not allowed to function as guides for us if we are in the physical and they are in the unobstructed.

It was quite a surprise for us to learn that we do not choose our guides, they choose us. "It is not your choice who becomes your guide, and this is so total objectivity can exist. Before you incarnate, while you are still in the unobstructed, you may have a good idea of who some of your guides may be." The amnesia of our spiritual awareness caused by the curtain being drawn ensures adequate objectivity after incarnation, even if we had such information while still in the unobstructed.

Mario gave some comments on at least one of the many factors involved in selecting an incarnated soul to guide, again using himself as an example:

What you frequently do is find commonality in your major area of study and that of the individual you are going to guide or represent. You see, I have chosen to put most of my energy into the psychological and physiological growth of man. If you studied my behavior in dealing with people and could label me, you would find that I am an historical social psychologist. I am involved with the social behavior of man, to teach how to become social creatures again.

As spirit guides, our usual and primary method of influence is by impingement.

A great deal of effort and energy is placed in impingement and methods of impingement—how to communicate with a physical mind. It is not difficult, really, to project an image, a thought, or word—that is, to send a message to the physical mind. We simply trigger the mental process by using psychic energy to transmit the energy involved with the thought process. The difficulty comes in the reception, and in the translation after it is received. What the mind does with it after it is sent we have little control over. The guides attempt to communicate with you in a positive way, trying to influence you without interfering with your right of free choice. Try that some time and see if it is not difficult. Try to give advice without taking away the right of free choice. It is almost impossible. Any time you offer advice you are influencing somebody. We must be very careful.

STEP FIVE

Step Five remains very much an enigma. For several years, responses to questions about this level were very general, such as "Most of Five is unobstructed work. It has to do with many things about the unobstructed, learning to really prepare yourself for Six and Seven." For some time, the only clear piece of information about this level was "you cannot exceed Five until you finish One." What this means is that an entity is "stuck" on Step Five in the unobstructed until he completes Step One in the physical. Only after completion of experiences in the physical can we move to Steps Six and Seven in the unobstructed. After persistent questioning, we did get a figurative peek through a crack in this usually closed door.

Five is the last step before you graduate into your upper-division work in Six and Seven. Five is almost like a test; it is similar to what you would do if you would have an examination, as in your finals. You would be completing your studies and taking your finals at the end of your degree work, to establish how well you have learned your material. What you do after this in the remainder of Five is your final evaluation of One, Two, Three, Four, and Five—an evaluation of all that you have studied.

STEPS SIX AND SEVEN

These levels are said to be roughly comparable to graduate studies in a university.

You combine your learning up to that point and take your experiences into the sixth level for condensed study and further expansion, very much like your lower and upper divisions in college. It is a very progressive thing. When you start into your upper-division work in one of your universities, you are in new fields of knowledge. But they are still related to the previous subjects that you covered. Is this not true?

In this graduate-level work,

You spend a considerable amount of time in other galaxies which have planets with intelligent life; you also study those

life forms and their systems. What you do primarily is communicate with entities in the unobstructed environment of
those galaxies. As man measures time, it takes a while to
reach these galaxies. They are many of your light-years away.

The purpose of these studies of other galaxies with different life
forms is to broaden our understanding and appreciation of the
Source's many ways of seeking change and expansion and of the
extremely intricate manner in which various energies function in
different systems.

In our study of energies and life forms in other galaxies, there
are occasions when we do not need to make direct observations or
experience direct communication. In such cases we might simply
check our own archives of knowledge or communicate with an entity who had studied that galaxy. "What you would be aware of is
an entity that had been there. They would communicate their
knowledge to you and this might suffice unless you wanted or
needed the actual experience of going there."

A special focus in Step Six is learning to apply our acquired
knowledge.

You could also consider the sixth level as similar to an internship in your hospitals. In internship you have your physicians
becoming familiar with the practice of physical energy, the
application of rules and theories. They have learned from
books, and now they are going to put their knowledge into
practice. They observe their seniors, watch the application,
and begin to practice their knowledge. The sixth level is when
you become very seriously aware of the application of your
previous studies. You delve into the relationship and correlation between the unobstructed universe and the Source of
Divinity, how the Source of Divinity relates to and with the
unobstructed. You become more aware of all the applications
and ramifications of the Source's laws that govern in the
unobstructed. You study the association of the unobstructed's
inhabitants with the Source of Divinity.

As Step Six is similar to a medical internship or to graduate-level study in a university, Step Seven is comparable to a medical residency or original research. It appears that Step Seven is the beginning of individual creativity in the entity, at least in the sense of adding something to the unobstructed. As Aenka described it:

You have a period of time in this residency of application to contribute to the unobstructed universe those things you have learned and gained. Naturally, you do this from the unique configuration of your identity and your destiny experiences. This is your contribution to the obstructed and the unobstructed universes and is a great achievement.

Mario also spoke of Step Seven as "writing what you call your dissertation."

You are creating, adding to the knowledge to be shared with the physical for scientific advancement and discovery in all areas. If you will notice, in technological advancement it appears to be somewhat progressive. You will go along with somewhat of a struggle, where there seem to be very few inventions or new discoveries or sharp changes in technology. However, there are periods about every ten years of your time when seemingly something extraordinary is discovered or invented.

He went on to say that one significant factor in these apparent jumps is the result of the Source and entities in Step Seven literally extending and creating new formulas for further expansion. The formulas are placed in the archives of knowledge and imparted to man through the intricate devisings of guides in selective impingement. This information is made available to the minds of individuals in relation to man's overall social and spiritual evolution. As Mario puts it, "They in the body struggle with something for perhaps ten years, and then the formula is provided in the

unobstructed to be impinged or discovered. The discovery itself is
by impingement or intuition."

There is one additional general thrust or theme of progressive
study/function through Steps Six and Seven. Whereas in Step
Three we serve as consultants and committee members to individual entities, in Steps Six and Seven we "are the lifelines, or
what you would consider governors."

> They maintain all of the procedures and laws that govern
> the unobstructed, causing it to be in complete relationship
> with universal laws which the Source of Divinity applied to
> govern the unobstructed. Steps Six and Seven, in these di-
> mensions, would be roughly comparable to your high courts
> in the physical. All entities on levels six and seven are the
> governors of entities that monitor the behavior of other enti-
> ties. Instructions to the unobstructed from the Source go to
> those on the seventh level. However, these entities have no in-
> fluence at this time on the Source of Divinity. The Source is
> the all-powerful.

The last aspect of Step Seven is final evaluation, and apparently
much time is spent in this process.

> Every experience you have had in all of the other six levels of
> your growth must again be evaluated. It is the final assess-
> ment of everything you have gained, all the experiences and
> all the growth possible; ensuring the Source will permit you
> to merge back, to go home.

Concerning the contributions we make to the Source beginning
with Steps Six and Seven, Aenka described them one evening in a
rather simple fashion.

> All of the energy or power you receive when you leave the
> Source, and all the gained knowledge and experience you ac-
> quire, you return to the Source after your progression of

evolutionary development. When you finish the seventh level you merge back with the Source. You could say the battery is fully charged and you are ready to go into the prime vehicle to do your job. You add to that which is the Source, you become another cell to strengthen the Source of Divinity and to contribute to further evolution.

How do we know when we have completed our individual evolutionary process? How do we know when we are ready to merge back with the Source, to return home? As Mario puts it, "Oh, you know. Do know when you are thirsty?"

CHAPTER THREE

The Obstructed Universe: Physical/Spiritual Beings

The great business of life is to be, to do, to do without, and to depart.

—Viscount Morley John

THE SPIRITUAL CHALLENGE OF PHYSICAL LIFE

In the early days of our darkroom experiences we did not think of physical life on a daily basis as an important aspect of spiritual growth. Like so many people, we assumed spirituality to be primarily related to more esoteric type of experiences or some type of enlightenment. We were mistaken.

Do not separate the physical from the spiritual. They are inseparable in the first step of growth. You cannot live in prayers, you cannot lose yourself in spirituality or religion. You cannot escape physical reality and physical responsibility by calling such avoidance spiritual, religious, or any contribution to the Source. Your responsibility in Step One is your physical being, your physical and psychological development. Deny your body growth, acceptance of love and understanding, and you are denying the plan of the Source of Divinity. Curse your body and you are cursing the Source, because this magnificent creation was designed as your vehicle in the first phase of your spiritual development. Oh, you shall deny it, you shall curse it, and you shall reject it many times, only to return to try again.[1]

Many people find physical life boring or unsatisfying, and emotional life frustrating or empty. It is not difficult to understand why one might attempt to "speed up" the experience of meaning in life by circumventing the physical and emotional in one way or another. We asked Aenka about the feasibility of working on other levels of spiritual growth while in the body.

I shall attempt to answer this without offending the belief of any individual living. While such endeavors could be many things, most often it is an effort to escape reality, to find the heavens and understand them. It is most often not intentional. The work such a person is hoping to achieve can only be done in the unobstructed without a physical body. I shall say there would be no point in an individual accepting a beautiful and marvelous body, nurturing it to health and growth to adulthood, only to let it sit in silence.

But would not such attempts, if successful, save time in overall spiritual evolution?

Heavens, no. It would save them pain if they could get along with the physical development and not ignore it, nor attempt to escape it through some search for a higher plane.

Many people may have difficulties of a variety of sorts with the idea of full physical living being spiritual. Some will be reluctant to believe its importance from an intellectual or attitudinal point of view, insisting that rising above the physical is the only true higher form of spirituality. Quite a few have specific fears and guilts regarding their bodily or emotional functions and are fearful of looking more closely at those aspects of their lives. In response to such doubts and reservations, Mario and Aenka hold steadily to the spiritual place of physical/emotional aspects of life.

There has been and will be great concern regarding physical destiny. It seems to many that on the one hand they must reject their physical body, holding to the hope they may gain spirituality. On the other hand, they may reject spirituality in hope they may endorse the physical. Either way is a most trying and most frustrating approach to heaven. It is like walking a tightrope. Why should not the physical body split off the tightrope and walk comfortably towards the pursuit of life's fulfillment? It is because everything that is beneficial or pleasurable to the physical body has been rejected or made to feel sinful. Nothing about your body or its functions is either dirty or sinful. He would not have made all of the magnificent functions of this physical body had it not been intentional and for the purpose of full expression. Deny your physical body expression of which it is capable and you will suffer.

For many who break through the conditioning and influences of some of their previous ideas of spirituality, it will seem reasonable indeed to consider that physical life is part of a larger spiritual process. Aenka explains this as follows:

The primary purpose of the first step is to develop physical growth. This entails all of the attributes, all of the qualities, all of the capabilities of the mental process. If all the qualities of your personality were in total rhythm, you would know aggression, authority, submission. You would know your spiritual facet. You would be able to satisfy all of the hungers

of the physical body both mentally and physically and to experience them at their fullest.[2] In completing Step One, you
are to experience complete and total physical experiences of
every positive quality to the fullest. When you go back to the
Source, you return to the Source all of these experiences.
This adds to the strength, to the power, and to the knowledge
of the Source of all Divinity. The Source is then stronger,
more intelligent to expand out to infinity, to other universes
and to set into motion other life forms, other ideas of
phenomena.

The ultimate purpose of physical life, then, is the same as that
in the unobstructed—that is, to gather experiences and integrate
them in our unique way for eventual contribution to the Source
itself. But how much learning and how many experiences are
enough? How do we "measure" gained experiences in the physical? The entities say we are to learn these aspects of living not to
any particular degree of excellence or elegance but to a level of
comprehension they call a "working knowledge" of any particular slice of life. As a soul, you are finished with Step One "when
you have completed all of the experiences the physical and psychological are capable of, experiencing and handling it well physically, psychologically, and emotionally. I would not have time to
count the experiences one must handle well."
Physical life is not only important but the most difficult of the
seven steps of spiritual evolution. When we finish this step, we
"have accomplished the most important step of the seven. It is the
most difficult."

Why is the first so difficult? Because of the experiences
necessary. All positive experiences of the physical must be
lived, every appetite satisfied, and they must all work in harmony at one time or the other for this to occur. You may in
all your past lifetimes have had only one pair of your emotions working in harmony. If you considered every facet of

personality structure and its opposite, and you only experienced one rhythmic pattern in a lifetime, it would take a
great deal more than your fingers to count the life incarnations necessary.

It should be emphasized that the task of Step One is to experience all the *positive* experiences life and living has to offer.
This does not include a need to gather destructive experiences.
Some people interpret the teaching of gathering all positive experiences to include malicious or destructive behaviors. "It is not
necessary to be destructive. You do not need destructive experiences to grow. You do not need to experience theft, murder,
or any other thing that is destructive or in violation of your fellow
man." Destructive behaviors lie strictly in the realm of
psychology and relate to spirituality only as challenges to be met
and confronted in our self-learning and personal growth process.

Although destructive behaviors cannot be rationalized along
spiritual lines, neither can the denial of anger. People who have
difficulty in dealing with emotions such as anger might see any
anger as destructive and thereby to be avoided, suppressed, or in
some other form pushed away. We asked Mario about this issue,
in particular about those people who might see anger as not
positive.

I agree with them in the way their mind works, that I am not
to be angry. But angry in what definition? Unnatural anger,
where you thrash or do your fellow man harm is not positive
but destructive. But anger is a natural emotion, and basically a positive force. It was designed to motivate constructive behavior and can be used to bring about change if it is
not allowed to become destructive. Man must learn the constructive and natural use of anger. It is a challenge to you,
and you will experience more integration as you learn to
channel this form of excitement.

What are the challenges of physical life as they relate to needed experiences in the body on our spiritual journey? How do these challenges interact with entrance of a soul into an infant body, psychological and physical growth, natural and unnatural emotions, destiny during one lifetime and over many lifetimes, intuition and impingement from the unobstructed, psychic energy, physical death and transition of the soul back to the unobstructed?

BASIC PERSONALITY TRAITS

*God obligeth no man to more than he hath given him ability
to perform.*

—Koran, Ch. 65

In the unobstructed we select a fetal body in which we will incarnate when it is born. One of the factors considered in making our selection is what the entities refer to as the "basic personality structure" of the fetus. Each human fetus is genetically coded through biological inheritance from its parents to have a particular configuration of the basic personality factors of introversion, extroversion, feeling, and thinking. Basic individual personality configurations differ in respect to the patterns of characteristics that are predominant.

There are four basic factors, or dimensions, of your personality: thinking, feeling, introversion, extroversion. These aspects allow you to function in a unique pattern psychologically and emotionally. Each aspect has an effect on your physical growth and the physical underpinning or structure of your psychological development. Your evaluation in the unobstructed would determine which basic personality structure you would select. You choose a body and would know before that body was born the basic personality structure it would have, based on these four dimensions. Thereby you

would know the predominant physical alignment of the personality—a thinking extrovert, a thinking introvert, a feeling
extrovert, or a feeling introvert.

It is interesting to note these basic patterns fit fairly closely with
some of the concepts of the eminent psychoanalyst Carl Jung.

Each basic configuration of these traits (what the entities refer
to as the *basic personality structure*) remains the same throughout
the life of that particular body. This is not to say that we function
rigidly in any manner or cannot and do not change throughout
our lifetime in how we function. The configuration refers only to
the *basic* style or combination of styles that we use in meeting the
challenges of life. A person who is primarily extroverted reacts
and functions differently from one who is primarily introverted.
A person who focuses more on intellectual reasoning will process
information in a manner differently from one who focuses more
on feelings or intuition.

While still in the unobstructed, we are aware of the destiny and
tasks we plan for our next incarnation. The choice of a particular
personality structure is part of our government-of-life plan in our
pursuit of this destiny. During some lifetimes one may choose a
personality structure (or parents, socioeconomic level, etc.) that
facilitates the task, but one may also choose in order to make the
challenge greater. Mario and Aenka explained that challenge and
destiny for any particular lifetime are the crucial factors in our
choices of basic personality types and parents.

Sometimes personality determines the difficulty or the
challenge to those things you hope to experience. If you had
failed in a previous lifetime in leadership or had not had the
opportunity to grow in authority, you would likely choose a
body that was introverted, for it would offer the greater
challenge. One would think if authority is what you had to
experience you would choose a body that was extroverted,
for to be a thinking extrovert would make it easier to be aggressive or to assert yourself. However, your choice is based

on challenge, and each time you fail you would make a choice that offers you a greater challenge.

Mario went on to describe a paradox regarding degree of challenge and likelihood of success.

The greater the challenge, the more apt you are to succeed. It does not appear that way. Those things that are easy for you usually escape you, because the body's mind and nervous system are designed to meet challenge. One will therefore choose something that presents a challenge. The greater the challenge, the more apt you are to accept it. Most likely you would fail if you chose and planned it to be easy for you, because you would put little effort into it. The things that are least difficult, you take most for granted. Those things that are the most plentiful become tasteless. The challenge must be there and the dare. It is natural for the human species to be dared before he can succeed, it is a part of the mechanics of pride and achievement. If a puzzle looks easy, you will not buy it.

It can be clearly seen in these comments as well as others that challenge is crucial to development in all lifetimes. If life is too easy, we learn little.

ENTERING THE BODY

Breathed into his nostrils the breath of life; and man became a living being.
—Genesis 2:7

If the fetus that we have selected appears capable of sustaining independent physical life and has the basic physiological personality characteristics that we seek for this lifetime, we can enter this body if no other soul has "laid claim" to it. *Laying claim* is a phrase the entities apply to the final choice of a fetal body by an entity. Once this decision is made, all other entities respect this choice and would never make an attempt to claim or enter that body. This dimension of respect does away entirely with any possibility of true possession by other than one's own soul.

Prior to birth and the entrance of a discarnate entity, a fetus has no soul. "Before a child is born, the fetus is a growth of the female body. It has no purpose other than growing into a human shape until the entity chooses the physical body and enters it." While many people may find the idea of a fetus not having a soul distasteful or irreverant, women who have miscarried, aborted, or given birth to a stillborn child may feel supported or reassured.

As far as abortion before the child is born, before the entity enters the body, to do away with that growth would be nothing more than choosing to remove a mole or other growth from your body because that is exactly what it is, a growth of the female's body.

It may appear that the entities are making a moral judgment about our values or decisions, but the authors do not think so. The entities simply state what they hold as a basic truth or fact and leave us to our own decisions.

I am not one to say abortion is good or bad. I am saying a female is entitled to choose to do whatever she wishes with the growth in her body. It is her personal body and her choice. Just like your body: it is yours and your choice who touches it and what somebody else may do to it. Your body is your own responsibility. No one can touch it without your permission. If they do, then they must suffer the consequences, and the consequences would be determined according to your rules.

Abortion from the point of view of the prospective mother is thus seen as a matter of choice based on priorities and personal values. From a spiritual point of view, no moral values are attached to the decision. But what of the entity/soul who may have been considering an aborted fetus as the physical housing for his/her next incarnation? The entities say this presents no difficulty or dilemma. The entity that had been considering that particular fetus would simply look elsewhere. The loss of that particular vehicle would not be experienced as significant. Time, as we measure it, is not crucial in the unobstructed, and there are many fetuses available as potential vehicles.

The attitude of entities toward a human fetus is not a cold, casual, indifferent, or disrespectful one. To them it is simply a fact that, prior to the entrance of a soul, the human fetus is no more than a physical organism, a possible vehicle. Entities have much respect and admiration for the remarkable physical abilities the body possesses and much appreciation of the Source for having designed this vehicle. Of course, once a soul inhabits an infant body, it becomes a being worthy of great respect. No other entity would even consider a casual or disrespectful attitude towards a soul-incarnated human body, for it indeed houses a tiny part of God itself.[3]

The entities describe the actual infusion of an infant body with spirit as a somewhat gradual process and use rather simple and at times humorous metaphors to describe it.

> The moment the child takes its first independent breath is when the entity enters the body to solidify. It is like a fertilization. You must solidify, take your place there, and give that physical form the experience of your presence. This entrance and solidification is what is meant by possession. *Solidifying* means time or experience. It is like saying how long do you leave an egg, in what temperature, before it solidifies? Or how long does your Jell-O have to be in the cooler?

The process of initial integration of spirit and body is apparently somewhat ticklish. One aspect of the difficulty seems to lie in the fact that after birth of the fetus and before final solidification, the entity can enter and leave the physical body somewhat at will.

It is similar to a fowl or a bird sitting on their eggs to hatch. If they do not maintain a temperature in a certain range, then the egg goes bad, does it not? So it is like an incubation period, during which you must stay in that physical body. The spiritual energy must be in the body a certain period in order for that physical body—the neurons, the development of the brain—to take the imprint for behavior and the potential for reasoning.

Mario's attempt to describe pictorially the solidification process provides a good example of the difficulty in translating spiritual or psychic processes into our less dimensional physical language. When a discarnate entity looks at us or perceives us, does it, for example, see our body and the spirit inside it also?

Yes, similar to a pea in a pod. Your essence, or your spiritual energy in ethereal form, is associated with the physical energy. It permeates your physical body. Then what it is like . . . how difficult it is to translate or describe . . . it is like the nucleus of a mass, a cell, but it has other components and other surrounding energy. The center of you—the entity, the Facet of Divinity—is located in an area of the brain you would call the upper forward quadrant of the medulla oblongata.[4] Now, can you picture putting a drop of water on a mirror? The water runs down the mirror and spreads itself into an icicle-like form. The nucleus of that drop of water is at the top, the rest of it spreading out, but it is all water. So, the soul is all through you.

Once a soul has accepted a body and solidified, that phenomenon occurs which the entities describe as the "drawing of the curtain." As previously mentioned, this phrase refers to our loss of a conscious awareness of our spiritual aspect. The awareness of having a soul that is a Facet of Divinity, all of our previous learning experiences in the unobstructed, and memories of previous incarnations are no longer freely available to us. "It was provided the physical mind would have no previous knowledge. That is what is referred to as the amnesia, or the drawing of the curtain."[5] The drawing of the curtain is purposely designed by the Source to increase the challenges of living in the body. Much of this amnesia is to remain for most of our physical lifetime, although there are some possible opportunities to see into the other dimensions and connect with them briefly.

When we enter an infant body, it is with the hope that this carefully chosen physical vehicle will carry us through a full life to a natural death. But what if it doesn't? What if the gamble of life throws us a curve and we die by accident as an infant or youth? The fail-safe design of reincarnation makes such events insignificant in the context of the evolution of a soul. We simply return to the unobstructed. With such an interrupted plan of destiny, we would only begin a search for a new fetal body earlier than we might have otherwise. The continuity of life proceeds.

A PHYSICAL/SPIRITUAL BEING

It is sown a natural body; it is raised a spiritual body. There is a natural body and there is a spiritual body.
—1 Corinthians 15:44

The distinction between our spiritual essence, which is the entity within, and the physical vehicle with its own personality orientation is meaningful and necessary but one that is difficult to picture and comprehend. In our body these two aspects are so tightly interwoven that we consciously experience only one awareness.

Try to separate in your thinking the difference between the physical processes and the spiritual energy which is you in your body. You, as an entity in your body, are aware at all times of what is going on, but you cannot communicate directly with your physical mind. You may well have had many physical personalities in various incarnations, but spiritually you have only one unique personality.

Mario described this distinction rather more pithily another evening.

You sitting there, that hunk of meat talking to me, is the *physical* you. It is not your entity, is what I am saying. I am trying to differentiate, to separate the you that is your soul from your physical being. It is your physical vehicle that is communicating to me at this moment. It is the neurological, the mental process of your knowledge you are processing and formulating. You as an entity are in there to accumulate experiences. The neurons in the brain are coded for you to behave and enable you to rack up experiences. You are in there taking a free ride. You are an observer. It is like playing golf and having a caddy: he retrieves your ball for you, he carries your clubs, he cuts the weeds; he does everything but hit the ball. You are gathering your experiences, but *you*, within, are not doing the labor. You are not initiating other than some preconscious maneuvering, and then only to the point that you do not violate free choice of the physical personality.

Could we, then, think of ourselves as almost like two beings in one body, one physical and one spiritual?

Yes, I would agree with that, but do not take it in a literal fashion and say that a person has two personalities. This could be misinterpreted and lead to many incorrect processes or confusion. Such has already happened to the point that some people are willing to write and record multiple personalities, multiple souls, or multiple bodies. . . . some believe you have a body for every thought you think. Just understand the physical body is the vehicle with which you, the soul, gain your physical experience.

One of Mario's main thrusts regarding the interface of our physical and spiritual aspects is that while we as an entity can influence our physical personality, there are definite limitations on how much and in what ways.

There are degrees of influence you as the soul, or entity within, have on the physical body's behavior. The more in tune the physical body is with the preconscious or the soul, the more apt it is to live in harmony. You are in communication with the spirit world by impingement and have an element of influence over the physical. But you cannot, as an entity, alter the course of physical processes, nor can you violate the choices of the psychological personality structure. You cannot reverse a traumatic event that was impressionable for the individual; the individual must resolve the issue through the physical and psychological faculties provided for him. So in many processes you as a soul in a body are helpless to offer the physical direction. Essentially, you are there for the experience. All of the universal laws and all of the inborn processes that apply to the physical will hopefully develop and perform rhythmically, that you in your body may acquire all of the experiences necessary.

EARLY LEARNING EXPERIENCES

At birth, aside from having a sexual identification, physical characteristics, and a basic configuration of potential personality traits, we are for all practical purposes a vulnerable new being ready for fresh learning. Our inherited characteristics and potential talents are still dormant, and our conscious spiritual awareness is obscured by the drawn curtain. It would be difficult to overemphasize the importance of the first few years of life as they affect our physical and emotional growth.

As infants and young children, we are literally at the mercy of our parents. Initially we need nourishment, physical care,

·warmth, protection, and security. Soon we will need the emotional equivalents of these as well as guidance for physical skill development. Training experiences are necessary in acquiring speech, learning appropriate social behaviors, and in dealing with our emotions, which at an early age seem to come from nowhere.

Our first few years of contact with our family contribute heavily to our basic attitudinal and emotional programming/conditioning. The basic attitudes toward life that we acquire as children become a blend of beliefs and emotions that influence our behavior throughout life. During childhood, many foundations are established for dealing with basic emotional reactions, self-concept, trust of others, and belief in oneself. Ideally, it is here that we begin to learn self-respect and appreciation for the uniqueness of ourselves and others, as well as begin to acquire social skills with a positive attitude and an appreciation of interdependence.

While the entities teach that limits and firm, fair discipline are important ingredients for healthy childrearing, they deplore trying to force children into any type of predetermined personality mold. They urge parents to support the uniqueness of each child—his personality traits, abilities, interests, and the like. One night, in responding to questions regarding the use of extensive behavior-shaping techniques with children to "produce" a predetermined personality type chosen by the parents, Aenka said, "That would be most harmful."

Some hope to mold the child into their likeness, and of course some succeed, should the child be innately organized for this particular attitude. It is hoped society will refrain from this sort of punishment—to force upon the child. The child must be offered opportunity for development in all areas, in hope his uniqueness shall reveal to the adult that which the child has offered to expose—his or her innate abilities. Do not judge uniqueness at a comparative level. Each individual shall develop uniquely.

PROGRESSIVE DEVELOPMENT

The entities describe four general developmental stages of social/emotional growth that unfold progressively through childhood and adolescence. These stages were designed by the Source in a sequential manner, each stage providing a rung on the ladder of development to provide sure footing as we grow. The developmental stages are given as autoerotic (0-1 year); narcissistic (1-5 years); homosexual (6-puberty); and heterosexual (puberty-death). The natural occurrence and full experience of the first three stages is emphasized as laying the groundwork for a committed adult heterosexual life.

Autoerotic refers to basic familiarity with, and pleasure from, the body and its functions. In a setting of security and safety—and, it is hoped, a lack of criticism for natural explorations—we learn that certain things feel good and bring either physical or emotional pleasure. We become familiar with our bodies as we enjoy the challenge of experiencing its capabilities. There is an inherent constructive naturalness of early hedonism. It prompts curiosity about the body and the world around us; and it involves intellectual curiosity as an instinctive desire to know. "Once you have experienced the autoerotic type of love as a simple physical basis for self-acceptance, you are ready for some expansion of self-acceptance."

The narcissistic stage refers not to vanity or distorted self-love as we think of it in adults but to an elaboration of acceptance and pleasure in the physical body and simple emotions, leading to more complex feelings of pride, a liking for oneself, feeling worthwhile. "Self-love, self-acceptance . . . you cannot be a healthy, active, social creature until you have experienced the narcissistic stage. And you cannot experience positive narcissism until you have had a healthy autoerotic experience."

The homosexual period of development does not refer to explicit adult homosexual acts but to the phenomenon of boys and girls of elementary-school age preferring to play and be with children of their own sex. It is a time of identification and exploration with others, a consolidation of feeling secure in self-worth and acceptance by peers.

That is the time when you learn to identify and be comfortable with your sexuality, to find pride and appreciate differences. Having and knowing the feeling of pride, the opposite sex is not a threat to you. Successful completion of this developmental stage leads you into heterosexuality.

Adequate heterosexual identity and healthy self-pride allows one to be fully aware of one's own individuality and uniqueness yet capable of experiencing interdependence. One learns to accept oneself, to acknowledge needs for others, and to interact in a sharing and mutually respectful manner. It is this stage, strengthened by the preceding three, that furnishes the confidence and personal security necessary to see life as a challenge rather than a threat.

All of these stages need to be experienced in a positive sense if one is to avoid basic distortions in self-concept and in ways of relating to others and to the environment in general. "It all has to be in each lifetime. Each incarnation, the physical body and the mind must develop all the natural processes of development for you to have those experiences as your foundation."

When we are children we need the acceptance and understanding of our parents to support our innate feelings and behaviors. Naturally intended emotional/social maturation involves learning to respect our feelings and those of others, as well as acquiring acceptable means of self-expression in relation to others. When we are young, we need support and guidance in our explorations. With gradually decreasing direct assistance from parents and other significant authority figures, we eventually become able to provide our own self-support.

The Four Personality Quadrants

Just as we have genetically coded developmental interests and processes that unfold naturally to foster our growth, we also have built-in equipment of a variety of sorts to assist in self-maintenance and constructive interaction with the environment. The entities speak of these numerous inborn tools as being organized into four major groupings, which they refer to as "the four quadrants": *physical, emotional, intellectual,* and *spiritual.* These correlate and interface in a number of ways with the four basic personality dimensions referred to earlier. The quadrants develop more or less chronologically through the developmental stages, generally in the order given. However, the primary importance of the quadrants is not so much when they arise as what they enable us to do as we meet the challenges of living.

The *physical quadrant* gives us an instinctual drive for survival, provides the sex urge, and works toward continuation of the human species. It includes the five senses, which allow discriminatory contact with the environment for protection and nurturance. From this quadrant comes the quality of positive submission, the acknowledging of physical realities that we cannot change or deny and that we need to come to terms with. Patience is a derivative of this quality. The quality of extroversion from this quadrant enables us to move about and contact others in the environment to satisfy our needs.

The *emotional quadrant* supplies a full range of natural emotions that support the innate desire to belong. The urge to find one's place, to be accepted and be a part of, is of crucial importance in learning socialization and interdependence. Healthy dependence and positive conformance come from this quadrant; a recognition of our need for others on many levels and the willingness to conform our behaviors in reasonable ways reflecting respect for others. Our feelings provide excitement and stimulation to add flavor, depth, and variety to our existence.

The *intellectual quadrant* offers us the ability to think and later reason, to use logic and problem solving as we move through life. Life is indeed a series of challenges and problems to be encountered and resolved. It is this quadrant that supplies our aggressiveness and positive nonconformity. These qualities are inherent in independent problem solving. Our physical and emotional quadrants assist our constructive aggressive attitude by supplying energy and drive to support us as we encounter challenges. Courage, the desire and willingness to encounter a challenge and master it, comes from this quadrant.

Our *spiritual quadrant* explores the universe within and without in attempting to understand the mystery of life. It is that infinite part of us which allows for contact with our entity within and the unobstructed, our tie to the continuity of life, and the meaning of physical life and destiny. It is the source of our intuition, directing us inward to reflection and awareness. It provides the matrix we draw upon for creativity, as well as the impetus to seek our Creator.

Two of the primary qualities of the spiritual quadrant are those of introversion—a hunger or striving to know our inner self—and independence. Independence is a necessary component for both life in the physical and our independent spiritual search in the physical. If we are to be true to ourselves, each of us must seek and find his own truth. To do so one needs the ability to stand alone when this is necessary.

From the four quadrants, if adequately supported in our progressive developmental stages, we as adults have access to all that we need not only to survive but to learn and grow. At times we shall feel overwhelmed with the task at hand, whether it be practical, personal, or spiritual. But the Source did not design our physical bodies accidentally, nor are they inadequate to face the tasks at hand. As has often been said, man *has* the ingredients. It is up to each of us to slowly work at integrating the parts we have in common into a unique self. We are a gift from God to ourselves. What we do with that gift is our gift to Him.

Natural and Unnatural Behaviors

*You are good when you walk to your goal firmly and with
bold steps. Yet you are not evil when you go thither limping.
Even those who limp do not go backward.*

—Kahlil Gibran

The entities speak often of natural emotions, natural and unnatural behaviors, and rhythmic living. They repeatedly point out
how fear, guilt, and greed disrupt the integration of our inborn
responses into a healthy and basically simple life. For example,
the importance of enjoying and relishing our bodies as well as developing and broadening our minds is frequently stressed. Yet in
most Western countries we all too often learn by cultural and individual distortion to feel shame and guilt about many of our
bodily functions.

According to the entities, the Source planned five basic emotions
to assist man in facing his incarnated challenges: love, anger,
grief, fear, and jealousy. Healthy use of these basic emotions at
any chronological age in our development, when integrated into
contact with others and the environment, is said to result in
natural behavior patterns. Such natural behaviors are constructive
and lead to personal growth, satisfaction, feelings of self-worth,
and harmonious living with others. These results may not be immediate, and natural behaviors may produce some interim un-
pleasantness or excitement. However, if motivation and purpose
are positive, and the process is followed through to completion,
the outcome will be constructive.

There are times when our behaviors are based on distortions of
natural feelings. This results in what the entities refer to as "unnatural behaviors."

What makes an act unnatural? It is unnatural to deliberately,
or with intent, commit an act that would harm another individual. Revenge is an unnatural behavior, the distortion of

the natural emotions of anger or grief. Any behavior detrimental to your growth or the growth of your fellow man is unnatural; it produces and creates a negative energy that will leave both persons uncomfortable. Neither person will gain any positive experience through unnatural behavior.

In many situations the issue is not clear-cut. It is often difficult in the immediacy of an interaction to determine just what is or would be natural or unnatural behavior. Such identification and discrimination has become more difficult as our society has become more complex.

At the time, a behavior may feel or seem to be very gratifying to you. However, if your behavior is causing pain to another individual, then it can only be unnatural. The exception to this is in instances where the individual is responding to your behavior through their own fear or guilt. They may project upon you their negative or unnatural behavior, wherein your behavior may not be unnatural. Hopefully you will choose to base your self-assessment upon the universal immutable laws that govern social creatures.

The immutable laws referred to here are ten universal principles designed by the Source to guide man in his struggles and choices in physical life; you will find them described on page 124. While these guidelines can be of assistance, the bottom line for choice and decision remains our own individual challenge. "Ultimately, it is for you to evaluate and allow your own wisdom to determine whether your behavior is natural or unnatural."

The entities would at times seem to use the words *positive* and *negative* in a way similar to *natural* and *unnatural*. "An unnatural behavior creates a negative environment or an unnatural environment. This usually causes disharmony or discomfort to the individual, whether you call it an unnatural behavior or act or negative behavior or act." We inquired about their concept of these words and got the impression that in a general sense they use them interchangeably.

However, more specifically, the entities use positive and negative in relation to *motivation* of behaviors, and natural and unnatural in relation to *degree of constructiveness or destructiveness* of the behavior itself. They steadfastly avoid morally loaded words such as *good* and *bad, right* and *wrong.* "The reason it is better understood in these terms rather than right or wrong is there is something so cruel and definite about such words. Right and wrong, or good and bad, have an air of superiority about them and are usually associated with an unrhythmic nature."

It might be helpful, in drawing this rather impressionistic picture of natural and unnatural behavior, to furnish an example of each in relation to one of the basic emotions.

I believe there is one natural emotion totally misunderstood by the conditioned human mind, and that is anger. Anger is very much a part of the instinctual survival drive. Anger in its natural state is an emotion that promotes aggression and very primitive behavior. When an individual becomes angry, adrenalin fills his system and he becomes very strong. He is ready to attack or defend the physical body. If the process were allowed to take its natural course in rhythmic behavior, he would never kill anybody. It would be instead similar to other animals you have observed: they fight until the stronger one wins the battle. The defeated one walks away with pride and the stronger one walks away with pride. It is natural rhythmic acceptance; the quality of submission whether one wins or loses.

Human beings are no different than any other species other than the fact that they have reasoning and a soul. The human being in a primitive and rhythmic state never kills his own kind. Fight, yes. Your friend and you might fight at the drop of a stick for some competitive reason, but the weaker one would always know when he was beaten, and the challenge would give him great pride. This has almost been captured, the meaning of this, in the ritual in which boxers come out fighting after the handshaking ritual. Hopefully both of them will leave the ring with pride and not with the feeling of defeat.

Distorted anger becomes hostility and rage. Fear, guilt, and jealousy become so much a part of it. When an individual becomes angry, rage and hostility can come in to support his anger, and the only thing he can think of is to destroy. Therefore he kills. You would think humans would have the ability to live a more rhythmic life and allow their emotions and natural physical hungers to guide them into a very progressive and constructive life, but we witness every day human beings killing each other.

EMERGENCE OF THE SPIRITUAL QUADRANT

Howbeit, that was not first which is spiritual, but that which is natural; and afterward that which is spiritual.
1 Corinthians 15:46

In a broad sense, our physical and psychological development from birth through adolescence can be looked upon as a three-pronged movement: (1) an unfolding of inherent physical and basic personality aspects, (2) acquisition of basic skills in dealing with thoughts, feelings, and our bodies for independent function as adults, and (3) an adequate degree of self-respect and pride in our uniqueness gained from love and emotional support by our family. During these formative years we are quite preoccupied with these issues in our lives and are usually not *consciously* aware of our spiritual quadrant.

The spiritual essence is at times recognizable in children, regardless of their degree of conscious awareness. The sensitivity of children to changes in their environment (internal and external) is well documented, and at least a part of this sensitivity is related to the spiritual quadrant. The flower bud of spirituality that will bloom in adolescence can also be seen in children's creative play and fantasy. These experiences help prepare the child to consider that reality and meaningfulness can occur without scientific proof and at times can even seem contrary to, or different from, our everyday physical reality. Indeed, the uniqueness of each child is a reflection of his unique soul as well as of his biological makeup and environmental influences.

The Source's design for progressive development allows for the first three quadrants to lay a firm foundation for the conscious consideration of the meaning of life and our part in it. With the emergence of the spiritual quadrant into consciousness, we begin to wonder why we are here, what the meaning of life is, who or what God is, what our purpose or destiny in this life is, and what we are to do.

> You are not conscious of the spiritual quality until its awakening, and this usually happens in adolescence. Then you can become one with yourself and wonder what you are made of. You wonder about the universe and your position in it. You wonder about the universal energy—the Source of Divinity. You become aware of your strengths and weaknesses, and you realize there must be something more powerful. There must be some purpose for this life. Adolescents and young adults begin to search to find the answers from within, to seek personal and private knowledge of spirituality. How harmonious this all is and how truly life begins to blossom! Life begins to have a deeper meaning for you as your spiritual facet begins to unfold.

If the spiritual quadrant does not unfold to consciousness until adolescence, what of early religious training? Is it of no avail? Surely religious ritual must fit into the scheme of things somewhere? Elaboration by Mario and Aenka of the time frame relative to the emergence of the spiritual quadrant brought to light a basic distinction of which we were unaware.

The entities are not saying that the spiritual aspect is *unavailable* to children and neglected by them. It is simply that children take this aspect for granted and do not realize its significance *consciously* or in a reflective manner. Children's thought is still very concrete at this time of life; their attention and interests are focused on their physical and emotional development. With adolescence comes a *conscious* awareness of spiritual issues and the development of questions concerning broader aspects of life. The spiritual flower begins to open to awareness.

A child before young adolescence is totally unaware consciously of spirituality. They express many characteristics of this quality and of course are primitively motivated by the rhythmic spiritual pattern. The conscious hunger to know of one's spiritual aspect does not manifest itslef early because during prepuberty experiences the focus is on total physical exploration of the physical world: the body, the mind, the intellect, emotions, the curiosities—to know and to explore these realities. Children are very much involved in the reality of their environment—real things that they can see, smell, taste, feel. That is where their hunger is so involved for the first twelve to fourteen or fifteen years. At that time the intellect is becoming well saturated, well pleased with its food, with its knowledge. And now there is room, and the need to search, for things spiritual. The universal law was designed that way because in adolescence the body is very near reaching its peak of maturity and growth, and soon it will start its deteriorating process. These hungers awaken according to design, to help you with gathering your experiences.

Please understand this is for the maturity of an individual, enabling them to become seriously concerned or aware of spirituality—to begin to explore the meaning of life and have a hunger to know. It is not that the adolescent or the adult is any more spiritually attuned or subject to spiritual experiences than children. It is just a factual progression. As the emotions, mind, and body mature in responsibility, the conscious hunger and instinctual urge to know develops. Children primitively live and accept experiences as such. They take it for granted, you see. If some spiritual or psychic experience that we might call profound happens to them, they will accept it, if the adult does not distort it for them. Other than that a child *lives* spirituality, they do not search for it. A child is spiritual in its natural behavior until they are trained or ridiculed out of it. The only thing the adult experiences the child does not is to take things more seriously, to consciously and purposely expound and explore. The child just enjoys the frosting on the cake.

Since one of the authors (Barham) had worked with terminally ill children, such generalizations served as an invitation for further questions. What about children who, after a long illness, approached death with peace and equanimity, sometimes speaking easily of the next life? This is referred to by the entities as a premature awakening of spiritual awareness and is spoken of as a part of the Source's fail-safe design to assist us in our transition through physical death, should death be imminent prior to adolescence.

Yes, if children are faced with death and are subject to the transition, there can be a premature spiritual awakening or hunger that triggers the needed experience or awareness of spiritual truth. Spiritual wisdom in a conscious and reflective manner, such that a child might possibly experience prior to adolescence, is a premature awakening to the continuity of life.

Such premature triggering of spiritual awareness ''comes about as a hormonal and neurological result.''

The developmental stages of the four quadrants of the physical anatomy are specifically designed in their development to unfold at different stages in growth periods. This involves hormonal, neurological, and other body-chemistry factors involved with maintaining consciousness in the framework of the nervous system and experiences of the environment. In natural progression the physical quadrant is the first to develop and the first to deteriorate; the spiritual quadrant is the last to awaken in development and the last to go before physical death. Now if the physical is permanently impaired critically or terminally, then it would almost be like a speeding-up process or acceleration, and the spiritual quadrant becomes the focal point. So some children become as little old wise men.

It is unlikely that conditions or experiences other than life-threatening illnesses might trigger a premature spiritual awakening.

It is possible, but not likely, that there can be a neurological mishap that would automatically trigger the psychic and spiritual processes to open the gate or raise the curtain that one may experience an unusual or premature spiritual experience. However, it is not likely a person through such neurological trauma would become more spiritual unless there were a need, such as their physical life being threatened.

Most of us do not consciously face the challenge of existential and spiritual issues until at least adolescence, as the Source's plan intends. The process of coping with emerging spiritual issues at that time in our life, compounded with the issues of sexuality and the conflicts of learning to stand alone while still experiencing some dependence on family, is far from easy. Adolescent turmoil in our complex society clearly reflects the difficulties of this time of multilevel change. Indeed, one may well be in one's thirties, forties, or even older before opening to the spiritual quadrant. This certainly is no aspersion on any one individual, but rather a comment on the obscuring complexity of our technological society. For practical purposes of understanding the issues involved and respecting each person's individual struggle, the word adult could be substituted.

The following quotation from Aenka, cast in a growth metaphor that has become very popular, speaks clearly of the quiet agony that underlies this transformational process. Indeed, struggle and confrontation with self and/or others is spoken of as almost a prerequisite for mature independence.

How would one go about explaining how it really is? We all know and have experienced the beauty of the butterfly. How did the beautiful butterfly become so? He goes through the agonizing growth in the cocoon. This cocoon, with its manifestations and development, brings about a need. Without a cocoon, the butterfly would not be so beautiful. The likeness of this is to the ability of the child to build a benign facade or shell for protection from birth to adolescence. This involves all of the attitudes this individual has learned from the trusted adult authorities around him. Without rebirth, the child would continue to reflect or mirror to society and the world only that which they have been programmed to do. This would be only dependence and conformity. So without fear and guilt, there is a need for rebirth, a breaking of the shell into freedom and a bursting into independence. Adolescents break their way through the cocoon just like the butterfly, spread their wings, become independent—rebirth of oneself, self-awareness manifesting in independence of free choice. What a magnificent thing! (Aenka, November 1976)

What about those of us who as adolescents or young adults do not have the confidence to claim our independence?

Sometimes this cocoon is too tough, it is difficult to break, so the butterfly cannot find the freedom. Therefore the rebirth is to become once again as the child, to be emotionally reborn in a safe environment enabling one the growth and development necessary to do away with all the fear, guilt, and negativity they have acquired.[6] So it was when Christ said that you shall be reborn and become as a child. So it is for you to be reborn and experience in a positive way safety and security with those you trust. Then you may break through the shell that encloses your understanding, to spread your beautiful wings that you may share your beauty.

The emergence of the spiritual quadrant into conscious awareness is heralded for many by a sensing of some purpose in life, even though they may not yet know what it is.

It is like the turtle, born in the sand away from the ocean. He does not know where he is. He does not know where the water is, or which direction it may be. Yet instinctively he begins to seek it out. Is this not true? It is similar to the human species. You have been endowed with a Facet of Divinity which is the entity within you, and in your puberty years or young adolescence you begin to instinctively seek out and pull towards the heavens.

The seeking of purpose and destiny is not an easy matter, nor was it intended to be. Like the turtle, we must start out in a general direction. Although middle to late adolescence is the natural time of spiritual awakening, some people do not have a conscious awareness of this experience until later in life. In contemporary society, the age at which one becomes aware of one's spiritual aspect appears to be related to many factors: cultural influence, psychological readiness, presence or absence of distortions in one's thinking or emotions, a lack of fear and guilt, a healthy feeling that "something is missing," and of course a willingness to approach this aspect of life on a personal level.

For purposes of discussing the implications of the spiritual quadrant in our adult life, as well as for the sake of consistency, we will adopt adolescence as the time frame for spiritual awakening. In our complex society this is an idealistic time frame; as actually experienced, the word *adult* could accurately be substituted in most places.

It is by means of impingement or intuition that we most often discover direction and purpose (destiny) in our life. For example, although it is true that some people choose a spouse on the basis of logic, most do so on the basis of feeling—that is, emotional or cognitive intuition. Or, we are drawn to a particular person or career and often have a hard time "explaining" our interest. Although you probably have an intuitive understanding of what is being described here, we would like to offer a few concrete examples from the authors' own lives. These will be couched in first-person narrative in hopes of injecting a note of sharing rather than of merely reporting.

MARTI: The awareness of impingement is now to me an exciting event; yet when I look back to adolescence, such awareness wasn't exciting. In fact it was unpleasant. Words such as *insight* and *impingement* weren't even in my vocabulary at that time. My childhood and adolescence were painful and difficult times. My natural mother and father divorced when I was only a few weeks old. My mother remarried when I was about seven years old. I never experienced much closeness or bonding to my stepfather, and he was killed in World War II when I was fifteen years old.

My mother, always a heavy drinker, began to drink even more. Living with her alcoholism finally became unbearable, and at age sixteen I left home. A great-uncle who was a Catholic priest helped me find a family to live with. I worked for room and board and continued high school. While this arrangement helped, it was still a difficult time for me. All my friends had mothers and fathers, fine homes, and the like. Denver, Colorado was a hub for servicemen. Many of my classmates dated and became very involved. I was shy, quiet, reserved, and felt alone.

One day, as I lay on my bed feeling a bit sorry for myself and my lot (after all, who really cared about what I did or didn't do?), words seemed to "pop" clearly into my mind: "If no one else cares, then *you* must." It has been many years since I first heard that sentence, but even now I can vividly recall the chill and surprise I experienced then. Somehow it made sense. I followed this message even though I didn't fully understand why.

Another time, I ignored a message and suffered considerably. At age twenty-two I was to marry for the first time—not a wise choice nor an unpressured one. As I stood before the justice of the peace and he spoke the vows that were to be repeated, I became aware that I *needed* to say, "No, I do not." My own fears of what people would think surfaced, motivating me to repudiate the impingement. These fears, as well as my own feelings of helplessness and inadequacy, held me rooted to the spot. I wanted to say no and leave that place. Instead, I said merely "I do." Such fears and feelings of inadequacy would be the basis of an unhappy marriage that would last three years.

As I gradually matured through many years via experience and personal therapy, I became more comfortable with such terms as *independence, awareness*, and *intuition*. Then I could begin to look forward to impingement/intuitive input. Although I'm now more open to such influences, I've never been able to predict or anticipate when they will occur and how. I do know that the harder I pursue them, the more they elude me. For me, the process is an allowing, and I can't force it. For example, a powerful impingement regarding religious beliefs occurred while I was driving along a freeway.

Religious teachings that I'd experienced as a child often perplexed and confused me even as an adult. The teachings of Catholicism offered much to me, but my continuing literal-minded childlike interpretations were limiting. For example, I couldn't come to grips with the concepts of hellfire and damnation. Something didn't ring true.

As I was driving along one day without concentrating on any particular subject—just watching the traffic—again there came clear words: "Does it make sense that God would destroy Himself?" This question hit me so hard I pulled off the road. I realized this wasn't merely a question but also an answer for me. Without a doubt I had a soul; without a doubt it was a part of God; and no, I wouldn't be destroyed.

As I assimilated my answer, I began to realize that although there are consequences for poor choices, I wouldn't be eternally condemned, punished, or rejected by God for them. Somehow I would "come home" despite my mistakes.

Other impingements I have experienced occur more subtly—almost as my own thoughts. I've accepted this and for the most part respond, having learned the hard way what I lose if I don't. My impingements have always pointed to positive directions, but I recognize that it's of my own choosing to follow when the time seems right. Impingement to me is a gentle nudge from out there.

Tom: I was born and raised in the South, and my parental family would be categorized as economically middle class. My mother and father were well educated but with little interest in the arts and none in psychology. What I now consider as a probable impingement occurred when I was about twelve years old and heard Hawaiian music on the radio for the first time in my life. Something about it attracted me, and for my next birthday present I asked for a ukulele. Believe me, there were *no* ukulele players in my environment. After I taught myself basic chords, I bought some sheet music with chord notations. My favorite pieces to play and sing were simple Hawaiian chants. I put my uke away at about age fifteen and thought nothing more of it. It wasn't until I was twenty-seven years old that I really even thought about those days.

During my twenty-seventh year I moved to Hawaii for my first Ph.D.-level staff job. As I was driving over the beautiful mountains to the state hospital where I would work, a feeling of incredible peace came over me. Somehow I felt at home. I don't know *for sure* if these two events are related. I do know for sure that Hawaii is one of only a few places I've so far visited or lived where I feel truly at home.

As an adult I've experienced what I consider two exceptionally strong impingements (or intuitions). The first was when I changed majors in undergraduate college from a combined degree in physics and engineering to psychology, this occurring when I was one semester short of a degree in physics. My father was a mechanical and ceramic engineer, and I'd always been good with math and enjoyed working with my hands. It seemed natural for me to follow in his general footsteps. However, I had the good fortune of having a very fine teacher in a required course in applied psychology. He seemed like a nice man who was truly interested in people. Shortly after this I also discovered a personal problem that scared the wits out of me. Rather than seek counseling or therapy (a disapproved option at that time), I began to read psychology books from the library.

I discovered psychoanalysis and the concept of unconscious thoughts and feelings affecting our conscious behavior. I was immediately fascinated! I dropped all my math and physics courses (consequently receiving failing grades) and spent most of that spring semester sitting on the front porch eating popcorn and reading psychology books. I was hooked. I'd never experienced any subject so interesting. By the time the semester ended, I'd decided to become a clinical psychologist and to try to help people with their personal problems. My parents were confused by this change in me but lovingly supported my decision, even though they disapproved of the choice. I've never regretted becoming a psychologist.

The last personal experience I'd like to share I think of as the opening of myself to my spiritual quadrant. I had reached my goal of the "American dream": the title of Doctor, a satisfying marriage, a pleasant, modest home, and success in what is paradoxically called private practice (I never could understand why they called it that; after all, we're open to the public). But lo and behold, after studying and working nineteen years to reach my dream, I felt empty. I enjoyed my work and family, but there was a cardboard taste in my mouth in my private alone time. I explored this problem in therapy but couldn't discover any underlying repressions or conflicts to account for it.

At about this time Marti and her husband, Jay, came to Hawaii with Elisabeth Kübler-Ross to conduct a five-day workshop called "Life, Death, and Transition." I'd never heard of the Barhams, and all I knew of Elisabeth was that she was trying to bring death and dying out of the closet. I figured since I was feeling in a sense personally dead, I might as well take a week off from work and go.

The first three days of this workshop I was most dissatisfied. I prowled at the back of the room, smoking and feeling critical. Everything I was hearing I was familiar with either through direct experience or reading. Then it happened. They began to speak of life after death, and I was once again "hooked." I was fascinated and allowed their influence to enter me. I exploded with excitement, and for weeks following the workshop I had a number of powerful, unique experiences that I consider psychic or spiritual. I was very confused for many months in sorting out ego wishes and psychological products from what I consider "real" phenomena and experiences, but I hung in there. In no way was I going to let go of this new part of my life, reclaimed after at least twenty-one years of denial and cynicism. I'm alive once again, and I feel more complete.

CHAPTER FOUR

The Obstructed Universe: Struggling for Maturity

Your daily life is your temple and your religion.
—Kahlil Gibran, *The Prophet*

SPIRITUALITY IN THE PHYSICAL

The entities love to talk about how our individual Facet of Divinity, once it emerges into full adult consciousness, has the potential of imbuing all aspects of our physical and emotional life with a special quality. However, for us in the body, awareness of our spiritual aspect can be not only elusive regarding direct experience, but difficult even to identify. In attempting to help us grasp the many aspects of spiritual energy that can assist us in orienting and organizing our lives, Mario and Aenka have taken many different approaches.

There have been many questions regarding spirituality and what it is. It is everything, everything combined with something else. It is a rhythmic combination of all the checks and balances of life. Every action that occurs shall be negative unless it has the quality of spirituality, anything from singing to sexual intercourse. Did you not know that intercourse is spiritual? I shall allow you your preference, to consider it spiritual or sinful. What does it mean to you? It is fun, but more than that it is one of the highest ecstasies man can feel. It is the very core of your physical drive. All of your physical hungers stem from your sex drive, your procreative drive. One of the greatest things is the love of your physical body. Children love the sensation of their body. They love the way they feel. Should this expression be allowed to develop in a natural way, they will continue to appreciate and love their body as they grow. All of the steps of growth a child experiences lead him into the developing and awakening of spirituality and then to the marvel of knowing and learning. What am I? Who am I? What am I here for? What is my brother like? What is my fellow man like?

Spirituality is learning about yourself and sharing your personality—the desire for expression, the desire to share your knowledge. Interdependence is a true quality of spirituality—to give, and a deep desire to give more than you receive. Have no fear of receiving, because as you share, every aspect is returned to you tenfold! Then you begin to feel your place in the universe. Let your spirituality be your rhythm. It is the beginning and end of all there is and all there shall ever be. There is no fear, no guilt, no laziness, no inactivity in spirituality. Everything you do can have a quality of greatness about it: always the positive feeling of growth and progress, moving forward, never letting your mind *dwell* on negative feeling. Anger is tempered by spirituality. You must be aggressive to live in society. You must be submissive. You must be extroverted and introverted to live in a society. The strength of your spiritual facet is determined by your ability to understand your fellow man and his needs, but most of all the ability to recognize your own needs and fulfill them—the courage to fulfill your own needs.

Most of us have probably at one time or another met someone who unfortunately seems to flaunt his spiritual/religious awareness or knowledge and who exudes a generally unctuous air. This kind of arrogance and would-be superiority has nothing to do with spiritual awareness or wisdom and is clearly a psychological distortion. This is not the form of "greatness" the entities refer to. Indeed, they seem to speak of the simplest things as being the most tremendously spiritual.

The birth of life occurs. Observe the growth of another individual. Have you ever observed another individual, young or old, attempting to master a problem and watched him succeed? The ecstasy, the elated feeling, can overwhelm you. You become totally involved with feelings of spiritual enlightenment. Observe a child learning to walk. Observe your feelings. You shall become overwhelmed with the intent of nature. All of these small things you begin to observe, and this helps the awakening of spiritual development—not to compare or judge, but to observe and comprehend with appreciation and humility.

An important task of living is to lay claim to the soul within, but this *must* be by free choice. It cannot be forced on anyone. Indeed, one of the greatest stumbling blocks that prevent people from developing their spirituality is outer persuasion, however well intended it may be.

You cannot force a child to understand his spirituality. You can teach them philosophy and teach them a great many fears and doubts. And, of course, you can teach them to make a mockery of their true spirituality.

INDEPENDENCE AND INTERDEPENDENCE

To be an adult who is centered in his uniqueness, with adequate honest pride to be his own person, is not easy. To be such in regard to one's inner spiritual feelings and search can be even more challenging. There are many pressures to conform not only to what and how others want us to be, but what to *believe* in from a spiritual or religious point of view.

Aenka emphasized the importance of personal psychological factors related to independence and the emergence of the spiritual quadrant, even if claiming one's own authority might defy or deny established authority.

A great many individuals develop adequately by the time they become adults. When adolescents begin to manifest spirituality, they begin to recognize their individuality or their independence. From this awareness they begin to trust the wisdom of their inner self. They have truly discovered the Facet of Divinity within them. This is when they begin to break away from the authority and the needed dependence that was placed upon and accepted by them.

Like a snake sheds its skins as it grows, the young adult will shed his psychological protective devices if he is emotionally supported, in order to develop his own uniqueness. Glory to this happening, and God help those to whom it does not come; for they shall live in frustration and self-condemnation until they have discovered their rhythmic pattern. They shall not only project upon others their own inadequacies, but others shall project their inadequacies upon them. It is with an unrhythmic existence that they take these projections and live in anxiety or anguish, solely because they feel frightened or guilty. Because they are frightened, they must strike out to feel some semblance of importance and security. Always remember yourself. You are responsible to yourself first, and then comes the quality of interdependence and the sharing of yourself. That is all you have, you know—yourself. It is not your possessions and your wealth that your neighbor desires; it is your knowledge, your wisdom, and that innate ability to share yourself. Let wisdom within guide you and free you from self- or other-imposed agony of life. The only thing you really have that is permanently yours is your choice. Make choices wisely, and pattern a feeling of justice behind every choice you make.

While the entities stress personal independence as necessary in the sense of doing one's own thinking and uniquely exemplifying one's own values, they do not speak of "doing your own thing" at the expense of another. Healthy independence is necessary to claim one's uniqueness and pursue individual destiny. Healthy dependence is also needed, for truly no single person can satisfy all his own needs by himself. Whether we like it or not, we need other people to provide certain relationships, feelings, skills, and a variety of commodities and services.

Experiencing healthy dependence as a child and learning independence in adolescence will by natural progression lead to an appreciation of and respect for interdependence. Reliance on social interdependence within a large group is a crucial aspect of any civilization. Personal acknowledgment of interdependence on an intimate basis is described as a basic quality of rhythmic living that we are to achieve in the physical.

Interdependence is a wonderful quality. You cannot live alone. It was not intended for you to live alone. You must live together yet retain individuality and uniqueness. Your genius will provide what the others have not, and their genius provides what you have not.

Interdependence is the ability to be social. The human species is a social creature, as many animals are social creatures. Man is born to depend upon one another for physical, psychological, and spiritual growth. The interdependence of the human species is central to cycles of development, and it is this you work with. Interdependence involves the ability to accept others as they are without comparing yourself with them. Compare not, lest you be compared. It is fairness of competition which you would like to possess. You would like to learn to develop your confidence to the fullest extent and learn to share it with others joyfully. You can learn to feel great joy in others' sharing their talents with you. To observe the joy of others could bring joy to you, provided that you do not feel they have something for which you have longed. It is very difficult for you to appreciate joy and harmony in others when you have a sense of loss for yourself.

The experience of healthy interdependence is interfered with if there is difficulty in claiming one's own uniqueness or differentness from others with a feeling of pride and courage.

What causes one not to recognize the importance of his unique spiritual facet within him? It is the crippling of their emotions psychologically. Some have allowed themselves to become so crippled they cannot experience interdependence. Why does an adult feel fearful? Because psychologically there are so many facets of the personality structure still arrested on the autoerotic level of development. It would be difficult to believe you are walking around in an adult body, fully developed physically, yet functioning on the level of a child. But does it not stand reasonable to believe that a child at a very early age who continually pulls away from authority and tries to adventure into the wilderness, only to be scolded, will be instilled with fearful anxiety of the authority?

This type of fear is learned. It is not natural development. It is forced upon the child to be fearful of both independence and interdependence. You have been made to feel insecure within your environment, and this fear becomes so intensified you do not allow young adults to cast it off. The shedding of one's protective covering would allow for further development of their personality qualities, forever to be free of whatever controlling, frightening attitudes taught them that would interfere with their adult behavior.

What of healthy pride in the sense of ego, and the distortion of arrogance that covers a lack of genuine pride?

Ego is the healthy feeling of pride in your individuality. Should it be rhythmic and naturally felt, it is wonderful to feel genuine pride. False pride, however, is always supported by arrogance, and it is negative to feel arrogant. False pride must be supported by arrogance because it has no value. Of course, it is fear that causes the underlying self-doubt. You must realize this subject is so difficult to speak of because it is so simple. There is little to know, really, about yourself. Without fear and guilt life is so simple. It is beautiful. When you see an individual who truly enjoys life, watch their movements, watch their faces, and you shall know. You shall feel the radiation of beauty from them. If you are in the presence of an individual frustrated with life, you shall feel their frustration and you shall feel uncomfortable in their presence. Arrogance is supported by the superiority of false aggression and false extroversion. Such people tend to build what they consider an ego more powerful and more destructive than one can imagine. Of course, in so doing they approach all those in life with an arrogant manner. The taste of arrogance is quite bitter. An arrogant person is a true phony.

The entities' focus on uniqueness in a context of interdependence prodded our curiosity about a variety of complementary type relationships. Interdependence can clearly be seen in many aspects of living and is certainly not a new concept. An employer needs employees as much as they need a job. A ruler needs people in order to rule. Groups of people in a social structure need some person or persons to articulate and support their society's rules; these persons in turn reflect, in their guidance, whatever major changes that occur. We wondered how the concept of interdependence would fit in the broad category of male-female relationships, and asked about differences between women and men as well as how they complemented one another.

MALE-FEMALE DIFFERENCES

One of the aspects of living that we all must deal with in every lifetime is our sexual identity and sexuality. There are of course many factors that influence basic attitudes toward the "other" sex and how we identify with "our" sex. The entities fully acknowledge vast individual differences in maleness or femaleness from a number of points of view, including a basic physiological one. Referring to our chromosomal makeup, they point out what has long been scientifically established: "The male is 49 percent female, and the female is 49 percent male." While acknowledging the tremendous influence of cultural and early childhood experiences, particularly in our present highly complex society, they insist that there are some basic differences between men and women and how they orient to life and to each other.

Aenka commented on current times, in which many women feel "less than" men if they choose a domestic lifestyle rather than a provider's lifestyle.

Cultural environment distorts the true meaning of femininity. Basic attitudes become distorted. Woman becomes frustrated and so disorganized she has little semblance to her true nature. Nor the male.

A woman's basically different abilities and characteristics "make her no less superior than the male."

Male and female are equal in importance, and different. However, psychologically there has become a great competitive argument over intelligence. Who is more intelligent? I shall say to you the male is no more intelligent than the female, or vice versa. Each have their destiny and as partners they have their destiny. Interdependence is the intent of each sex as they seek a natural rhythmic balance. Should female strive to be identical to male, what purpose would it serve either? Interdependence, beautiful interdependence: one dependent upon the other for support, for comfort and safety, equally believing in their own destiny, equally believing in their own unique gifts to offer the other. Each sharing with the other their uniqueness.

It would be easy to read chauvinism and superiority into the teachings that follow about basic male-female differences, but such perceptions would truly be in the eyes of the beholder rather than the entities' statements and intent. They insist upon equal respect for both sexes and have little use for either male or female stereotypical behaviors—the macho man or the helpless woman. To fall or be led into such distorted and stagnant orientations will most certainly deny either person some of the more supportive experiences we all need. For example, is it a form of healthy or unhealthy dependence for a woman wanting at times to be held and feel protected? Is it natural for a woman or a man to want to be comforted?

Heavens, yes. But you would feel guilty for wanting it, because you would think you are a sissy, or weak. You should not feel guilty. You must realize both male and female want to be coddled. Would it be fair for the one and not the other?

The entities frequently use primitive man in a historical sense as a reference point in their comments on the potentially beautiful interdependence of basic male-female differences. It appears that what they refer to as natural functions of men and women, as well as basic distortions of these functions, are easier to point out in that remoter time frame than in our contemporary one.

The entities teach as a basic fact that each soul remains the same sex through all physical incarnations and in the unobstructed. While this is contrary to popular belief, it seems to have a biblical corollary in the statement "Male and female created He them.'' What does this mean to us in the obstructed through our incarnations?

In a primitive situation the female takes the mother perspective in the realm of understanding. Women are much more sensitive to, and understanding of, human behavior; and their inner wisdom is much more socially inclined to understand needs and hurts. The female would be more inclined to live in sensations and feelings and to leave the thinking and providing to the male. In primitive man, the male is the stronger physically. His time was spent outwitting and outdoing his prey. He must outthink the deer, must trap the fox. He must lure the foul. He must challenge the task of planting the tree for fruit. Of course he enjoyed it, because he must survive to win. If he is not acting, he is thinking, contemplating, dreaming of ways to outmaneuver. He spends a great deal of time in the intuitive to draw upon primitive wisdom to guide him. The female is much too busy with things at hand, but this does not cause her primitive wisdom to become any less important; she uses it in her daily tasks also, to protect and comfort.

Psychologically the female is much more adaptable than the male. In crises the woman would be the one most protective. The female would cower and instinctively protect her young with very little fear for her own life. The male, the provider, the physically stronger and aggressive, is always stimulated with fight or flight. The male would run if he could not fight. A woman is a mother, physically and psychologically, and cannot be compared to the male. Those primitive differences never change. The design is for interdependence, not identical behaviors.

As we talked further with the entities regarding spiritual aspects of personal growth, particularly in regard to male-female relationships, interdependence was repeatedly emphasized. Indeed, the innate desire to be a part of, to share, to give and take in so many ways, was intended by the Source to pervade much of existence.

But what of sex, since we are speaking here of male-female interdependence? Surely sex is an interdependent behavior. What is
the relationship of spiritual experience or growth to sex, if indeed
there is any?

Sex

The entities speak of sex as natural and healthy adult behavior
intended to be openly enjoyed in a monogamous and committed
relationship. They are critical of most of our societies' attitudes
towards sex.

To a greater or lesser degree, nearly the entirety of mankind
has been made to feel some discomfort about their bodies
and sexuality. Deny your body full expression and you will
only need to return to try again. This is one of the major
issues that necessitates your returning so many times. You
cannot hope to find the rhythmic pattern until you learn total
love, and this includes acceptance of your physical body with
all its natural hungers. The attitudes of your parents, your
culture, and your religious training cause your emotions to be
in conflict with your intellect regarding your body. You may
say you are very broad-minded and sexually liberated in your
thinking, but your bodily responses are governed by your
emotions and psychological frame of reference.

The culture of the United States in particular was singled out as
misleading people into confusing love, emotions, and sex.

Sex is a physical phenomenon and nothing more than that. It
is, of course, the highest form of pleasure the physical body
can experience. Most societies, and especially your society,
are so crippled in this concept because they try to make sex an
emotional reality rather than a physical reality. You try to
live on love in an emotional sense and you find yourself fail-

ing in a physical sense. The courts are filled with divorce proceedings because of it. Females more than males fail to achieve sexual gratification because they are trying to achieve it from an emotional sense. "If I loved him enough, then I could respond" . . . "If he loved me enough, then he would please me." Many do not recognize fully the development and importance of the sex drive and do not realize it is the physical body they have not taught. A male or female that cannot offer pleasure to their own body in a sexual sense can usually not be gratified or satisfied in an emotional sense. So it is for the individual to understand the physical, and to understand that sex itself is a physical phenomenon.

Knowledge of one's body and of what brings pleasure is described as essential to a satisfying ongoing sexual relationship. Applying this knowledge in a relationship is said to provide a firmer foundation for sexual satisfaction than pinning one's hopes on emotional feelings alone to provide the crucial key.

It is like driving a car. If you have never learned to drive a car, when you get in it it is very strange to you. Because of your programming as a child, you may have been taught never to touch yourself and never to think about it. Never let anybody else touch it because it is sinful, dirty, or nasty. Then you become an adult and fall in love. All of these dirty, nasty things that you are not permitted to involve yourself in are suddenly supposed to give you great ecstasy and meaning. Of course this does not happen. Males are taught to seek conquest; and the more conquests, the better, the more masculine they are. Few of them ever really learn how to please the female body, because they know nothing about it. And why they know nothing about it is because they have never experimented with it.

While the entities encourage experimentation and respect individual choice regarding dating and male-female relationships prior to an adult commitment, they urge discretion and judgment concerning intercourse prior to commitment. One reason for this is that intercourse is not seen as absolutely necessary in order to determine sexual compatibility.

> During the courting period, if an individual is natural, free, uninhibited, and does not play manipulative games with the other, all commonality and compatibility is usually sought out. This does not necessarily include sexual compatibility. It is highly unlikely that any one person in a physical sense could not enjoy the physicalness of sex itself with any normal physical body. There will be a certain amount of exploration and curiosity. But after the age of puberty, it is natural for female and male to become so prideful of their body they would not choose to be promiscuous. They will, however, be terribly in and out of love. There can be a number of healthy, natural love affairs prior to commitment.

The entities also speak of abstaining from frequent precommitment sexual intercourse for reasons of self-worth. Self-esteem, they assert, precludes such an exaggerated need.

> If you have no attitudes interfering with the natural behaviors and natural desire, the natural hungers; and you have nothing that has interfered with the development of self-love and pride; the physicalness of sex would not be needed to give one the sense of acceptance, humility, pride, and self-worth. You would have no need for the ecstasy of intercourse to offer you a sense of self-worth. How many pleasures are there to enjoy with "friends" other than intercourse? A multitude of things. You could in fact live a full life without intercourse, but not necessarily without orgasm.

This last observation seems to suggest that the entities might view masturbation as a practical and natural way to learn about one's body and its sexual responses—and to experience pleasure—

without being promiscuous in intercourse. In the following quotation about natural and unnatural sexual fantasizing, the same thrust can be seen.

Fantasy is natural; it is a natural process of life. If an individual is pleasing their own body, fantasy can be very productive and very natural. An example of unnatural or unhealthy fantasies would be that you required fantasy of a previous lover to reach orgasm with your mate. If this occurred, you need to examine your relationship with your mate and begin to work towards familiarity of your mate's personality and body. Learn how to promote an attraction that is favorable so that you can eliminate fantasy of others with your mate.

Mario has some simple and practical suggestions regarding enjoyment of our bodies and sex.

There is not another thing that causes disinterest more often than a body which is not thoroughly cleansed before lovemaking. It is not to say the natural secretions of the body are not pleasant. On the contrary, they can be very erotic. However, when they are exposed to the air for a period exceeding two hours, bacteria begin to form and the odor becomes unpleasant. Cleanse your body thoroughly, and anoint it with a pleasant fragrance. Many males feel it is only the females who should prepare their bodies in this manner. Make a nightly ritual of bathing your body and making it as sensual and desirable as possible. Making this one change will bring more creativity and spontaneity to your lovemaking.
Sex can involve all of your physical senses: taste, touch, smell, seeing, and hearing. So taste each other, learn to enjoy to touch and be touched, smell good for each other, leave the lights on so that you may watch your partner's pleasure and enjoy the designs of the body. Allow yourself the freedom to voice the beautiful sounds of lovemaking. The natural sounds which come during orgasm are stifled by many individuals due to embarrassment. Good Heavens! They would

not want anyone to know they are actually enjoying it! So they lie there and orgasm as unobtrusively as possible. It is like sneaking a cookie from the cookie jar. You have to quietly and hurriedly enjoy it before someone finds out what you did.

The entities are clearly in support of sexual experimentation within a committed relationship and speak of sex as potentially a satisfying and exciting challenge of a positive sort over many years.

Your sex drive is one of the highest ecstasies the physical body can experience, but it can become very dull unless you challenge it. Unless you enhance it by exciting experiences and continue to allow it to grow, it will become monotonous. Excess can also lead to monotony. The physical mind becomes bored if it is forced to dwell on the same thing for any length of time. It is continually reaching out to expand and grow. Do not allow it to stay in a rut.

It hardly needs saying that orgasm does add to the sexual experience and that it helps considerably in preventing boredom with sex. Indeed, orgasm is described as intended by the Source to serve such a function as well as to provide what is said to be the maximum physical pleasure of the human body. Orgasm serves the functions of providing physiological release of tension, aiding in the emotional bond of a committed relationship, and increasing interest in lively sex as a means of furthering the continuity of life via procreation. Mario broadened his comments on sexual orgasm to include orgasm of *other* parts of our body. He describes many types of physical orgasm, all natural and healthy processes that can feel pleasant if we allow them.

What is an orgasm? It is a physical phenomenon. There are many processes of the body that reach orgasm. The tongue is a very beautiful and healthy organ, and it has an orgasm every time it savors the expertise of a good chef. The variety of flavors and combinations of flavors offer that organ, through the taste buds, an orgasm probably more frequently than any other organ of the body. The upper respiratory system has its orgasm when it sneezes. What you call a bowel movement can be very pleasing, because it feels good.

There are many functions of the body that keep it healthy. These orgasmic processes and pleasurable processes have been incorporated into the sensation function so it would not be taken for granted. Meaning that if certain processes were very painful and traumatic, you would not readily move toward them and so the body would suffer. You would deny its needs, its processes. How many people do that? The bowel builds up a tremendous amount of gas, but to pass wind has been taught to be vulgar. When you block it, it begins to cause pain and do damage to the colon and the intestine. This same attitude is passed along to other functions of the body, even to the point of reproductive organs and their natural function.

Orgasm is so misunderstood and sexuality so distorted, the human being has lost the ability to accept the naturalness of that function for good health. So the natural process is constantly used *against* rather than *for*—to punish the body rather than to assist. Deny expression and your body suffers a loss of energy, and this causes a deterioration. Unfortunately, in your culture, even if you change your attitude to give yourself freedom of expression, you may suffer emotionally from learned guilt. Other parts of your body will then suffer as a result of that. Until man understands and accepts the natural processes, until they accept the natural hungers of the body, they will continue to suffer the consequences physically or emotionally.

From a historical point of view, women are said to have been more sexually aggressive than men. This changed as man gradually altered woman's open acceptance of her sexuality.

Unfortunately, in a distorted manner, man became shamed by the seductive nature of his female counterpart. Efforts began on the part of the male to tame the female, knowing not what he was to accomplish by suppressing the female into a submissive and fearful attitude. She began to reject all recognition of her true sexuality. From the beginning of these distortions she began in defense to use sexuality in a devious manner, to prostitute these qualities to keep the male in line. Since the female had no choice to express her sexuality freely, she began to use it as a weapon. She began to use sex for power, starving the male, influencing him to yield to her demands. She began to place the price of sexuality so high the male could hardly bear the burden. Forever after she has prostituted her loveliness in lieu of selfish gratification, and in some cases to deny entirely any personal desire for gratification. It is a wonder that the male caused it all and brought a terrible burden to both sexes. This shall be rectified in years to come. Few females of your day really experience or feel the true primitive feelings of their sexuality. It is so frightening to them, they would feel ashamed to recognize it.

Concerning the issues of sexual dominance or aggressiveness in our current society with reference to male/female behavior and attitudes, Mario speaks in a paradoxical manner.

It is a matter of how you would interpret what aggression is. The female in your society is still the aggressive, seductive entity. The making of rituals to attract each other—flirtation —is a natural manifestation of human behavior, particularly for the female. However, the attitude comes in that makes the male the culprit. You lead him up to the hayloft and then he is supposed to take over and seduce you. If you do not take it out of his pants, then he is supposed to do it. Then it can be all his fault, and that makes him the dominant person responsible for the sex act. That leaves the male in the eyes of society as the aggressor, and leaves the male with a feeling of

authority and power. What is it that you call it, the mach-
ismo, the distorted pride of his manhood—"I got a little last
night." But I will tell you, the female seduced him. Of course
there are situations when there is psychosis involved, when a
man has a problem and he literally rapes, but we are not
speaking of that now.

The entities' attitude that sex is intended to be naturally enjoyed primarily in a monogamous and committed relationship is
unshakable. They relate monogamy to both psychological and
spiritual growth, with the focus again on interdependence.

Mating is in the natural behavior of many species. If you
prostitute this energy, you are denying yourself or robbing
yourself of the energy to promote and motivate your
behavior to seek out a commitment. When you have sought
out and found a compatible opposite, you have a desire for
commitment. After the commitment comes the responsibility
for each mate to pursue a harmonious relationship, a sharing
of each other. This becomes a learning process of how one
can share with the other in the highest form of ecstasy in a
physical manner. That is why the element in your natural
behavior is called monogamy.

Understand, monogamy is a natural behavior and desire in
the human species. If you violate that natural element, you
will have unrest in the psyche. The discomfort may not
always be recognized and will not always be necessarily pain,
but it will manifest itself in a proportion that will cause considerable unrhythmic behavior. Any unnatural behavior that
is continued will manifest itself in an exaggerated state until
you become unrhythmically balanced. Then you begin to suffer neurosis.

What of those people who do not find sexual satisfaction with
their mate? The entities' first counsel is, of course, to work with
the problems openly and fully, with professional assistance if

necessary. If there is no resolution after much effort, what then? Continued abstinence in a relationship is not encouraged; nor is promiscuity, such as a superficial affair. While they do not encourage divorce, they do point it out as one possible solution. This is said to violate no spiritual guidelines if one has exhausted all reasonable possiblities in finding compatibility. While commitment is said to be a needed experience in physical life, there are apparently some subtle aspects relating to its achievement and even its definition for each individual.

> A commitment has no specified time and date. A commitment simply indicates the desire and willingness to take responsibility in working towards fulfillment in a relationship. If two individuals find themselves incompatible, then naturally they would choose to free themselves from the commitment. Aenka has phrased it, "So long as you choose to be together." He said nothing about forever and ever. You must take into consideration that you have the right of free choice.

While the entities do not seem to disapprove of sexual experimentation prior to a committed relationship, they clearly teach that promiscuous sexual behavior prior to or outside of a committed relationship is a misdirection. They speak of promiscuity not in terms of value judgments but simply in terms of consequences.

> To overtly share yourself *superficially* in an intimate physical way as an adult is not positive. It gains you nothing. You have not thereby gained anything positive towards your physical growth. Also it diminishes physical pride that you take in yourself or the self of another human being. It would be nothing more than going to your corner drugstore and having an ice cream. It is less fattening, of course, but emotionally and spiritually the repercussions of this experience will usually add to a negative reaction. Why? Because it is unnatural behavior. Any time you experience unnatural behavior, it does not sit well with body chemistry.

We have talked about many things having to do with unnatural behavior—nothing more: *unnatural*. You would suffer the same repercussions from promiscuity in an adult homosexual relationship as you would in heterosexual relationships. It has nothing to do with right or wrong, or good or bad. It has to do with natural laws, the universal laws which govern behavior. Any time that you violate natural laws you suffer the consequences. The consequences for promiscuous acts of intercourse for sheer physical pleasure alone are usually anxiety, unrest, or disappointment. You always fall short of the ecstasy that is hoped for. You've cheated yourself, misused the energy and the chemistry for which these feelings and desires are intended. Desire promotes the chemistry, behavior, and emotional reaction to motivate an individual to seek out a mate. Understand, to seek out a mate. So long as you choose to gratify your hungers in a superficial way, the likelihood of your ever committing yourself to one is very slim.

Aenka and Mario both referred often to some of the predictable and interpersonal results of not understanding and accepting sexuality as a physical pleasure that can add to the bond of a relationship. In particular they focus on confusing sex with love or turning it into an emotionally loaded or semisacred behavior. The inevitable result is to interpret emotional love in a sexual context.

Sex has been culturally programmed into you to represent love, and you accept this. Often when you are saying *love me*, it means *be physical with me*. How many of you use sex itself as a symbol of love? "Make love to me . . . love me." Every other word you use when you are involved with love is probably associated with some sexual connotation. Sex has been used to determine whether or not somebody loves you. "If she loved me she would go to bed with me!" . . . "If he loved me he would try and make me, even though I am afraid of it and I don't want him to." But if he does not try, then that is rejection; "He doesn't love me."

Aenka went on to describe how these confused attitudes concerning sex in relationships can lead to manipulative behaviors and other distortions.

So you begin to play games with each other. He does it because he wants her to iron his shirt. She does it because she wants a new dress. You begin to prostitute yourselves to gain what you want, you no longer do it just for the pleasure. So sex becomes a tool or a weapon by which you can gain what you want. It is so unfortunate that sex and love are used to prostitute yourself for personal gain. Love is a giving. It is the ability to share with others your own personal genius. If you give a person a gift, when it leaves your hands the pleasures that the other has with it, in whatever way they choose, is theirs. In your giving, if you have something attached to it, then it is truly not love, it is prostitution.

Then what is love? we asked.

LOVE

Love gives naught but itself and takes naught but from itself. Love possesses not nor would it be possessed; for love is sufficient unto love . . . love has no other desire but to fulfill itself.

—Kahlil Gibran, *The Prophet*

The entities speak often of love and its importance in our spiritual evolution. They describe this elusive phenomenon beautifully from many points of view as a mixture of feelings, attitudes, and behaviors. In its fully developed form love is unconditional, not tied to any conditions or manipulations, given freely in a sense of sharing. The entities differentiate sex from love in regard to their functions and origins, but they speak admiringly of those who are able to blend these different aspects of life in a committed relationship.

To present their many different teachings on love in an integrated manner would be difficult. Rather than attempt this, we chose to group their comments and use many quotations. Perhaps this may convey in some sense the beauty and importance of love and at the same time allow each reader to make his own integration.

There are many definitions for this word. Your greatest prophets and philosophers have tried to describe it, yet it continues to elude them. Love is a combination of a million facets of your personality. Attempt to pinpoint it and it shall laugh at you. I shall attempt to guide you on what it is and is not. It is not selfishmess. It is not suffering. It is not ecstasy sought for oneself. It *is* the desire to help fulfill this ecstasy within another. Love in the truest sense is *allow me to please you*. Often we have heard the words "Christ is love" because this was his objective. I am loved by your acceptance of me, you are loved by my acceptance of you. That is love.

Mario spoke of the expression of love as a transaction involving behavior as well as attitudes and feelings.

Shall we put it in very simple terms? To define love would be to have an affectionate feeling permitting an act of favor towards someone. It is very difficult for words to describe the transaction of the meaning of love. Do not confuse it with needs or wants or desires. Do not confuse it with physical and emotional heartbreak. How do you indicate to a person that you love them? Love is a movement. Love is an act. It is a behavior. It is a transaction. The other does not have to be aware of it to make the transaction complete.

While the entities teach that one can love without being "loved back" in the same way, they also speak of a shared or mutual loving experience in glowing terms.

The most magnificent feeling love has to offer is when you are sharing yourself with someone else. Many of you have captured this feeling. To share something with someone and to see and to experience this feeling.

CONFUSING LOVE WITH OTHER EMOTIONS

If love is so simple, why do we have so much trouble identifying, finding, expressing it?

Love is often confused with emotional feelings. If someone is causing you to feel comfortable emotionally or physically, it is easy to interpret that as love. "You make me feel so wonderful. You make me feel beautiful." What you are often saying is, "You please me." Let this pleasure be taken away, let them withdraw that, and then how do you feel? Do you feel angry and hateful? This happens most often when one denies their own hunger for emotional and physical gratification. When these hungers are not satisfied, they can be easily transformed into the interpretation that your lack of satisfaction is due to someone withdrawing their love for you.

CONDITIONAL LOVE

If we are not able to differentiate love from our basic emotions or physical self-satisfaction, we are likely to move into at least two misdirections: manipulation to gain love, and placing conditions on our giving to others.

If a transaction of love is permitted to complete itself, there can be no anger, no resentment. If the transaction is an act of prostitution or manipulation, then it is only a conditional act under the disguise of love. If you give a friend a gift, it is an act of love, providing you do not have any claim or conditions with your giving. How would you feel if that friend took the gift, put it on a rock, and smashed it with a hammer? Would that disturb you? Would it negate your act of love? It would not unless you have conditions, and if love is conditional, it is not really love. It is a manipulation, it is prostitution. "I give you something if you give me something." You have not initiated a transaction of love, you have attempted to manipulate a transaction of love.

"I will love you if" . . . "I will hug you if" . . . "I will give myself to you if." The word *if* has crippled more minds than all the words in your dictionary. Love has not conditions, because love is giving and sharing. I would continue to talk with you and to share with you if you were angry with me, even if you hated me. I would respect you for that, but I would continue to share my love with you, so long as you permitted me to. I ask nothing for it. My only reward is that act of love; and if this initiation or this act is completed, then I have loved. And if I have loved, then I am blessed. I am blessed by you for accepting and sharing my love.

THE ABILITY TO LOVE

Ideally we acquire the ability to love in our youth by being loved ourselves. Learning that we are loved helps us feel lovable and leads to self-love. When we love ourselves, it is easier to offer love to others unconditionally.

You cannot love unless you have felt love, nor can you continue to love unless you have an abundance of love. You have heard many times the phrase or the saying "Give from your overflow." Of course, an individual who has felt love and feels lovable continuously replenishes his fulfillment and has an endless measure of love to give. The absence of this is what keeps an individual from giving love. They give with strings attached. They shall set a cup of love on your doorstep only to set a larger empty cup beside it with a string attached. If their cup is not filled, they shall take back the smaller cup that they have given. This often shows up in criticism of your fellow man's behavior. You love him *if* he behaves in a certain way. "I have done so much for him, I have worried and been so concerned about him, and look at what behavior patterns he has!" . . . "I have done all I could and more, but look at what he is doing in return." So you begin to pull the string back; your cup has not been filled.

Love is not a privilege to be conditionally granted by man. It is a God-given right to experience love. You cannot experience understanding until you experience love, and this love will hopefully be experienced from birth to adolescence. If it is not, the mind is often crippled, and it is then most difficult for the adolescent to change into adulthood and live successfully. All of the potential rhythmic patterns that could have been developed begin to take a negative aspect.

While Aenka and Mario both stressed the influence of experiencing unconditional love as a child, they are reassuring that one *can learn* to love as an adult if one did not have such earlier experiences.

You never become too old to receive love. You are never too old to learn how to give love. But first you must love yourself. Love every fiber of your unique personality and body. Inspect your body, and think of all it does for you. Without it you could not exist, you know. I would like for you to learn about your marvelous body functions and the way they perform. How magnificent the body is, how beautiful it is.

LOVE AND EMOTIONAL PAIN

It appears love is always expressed as desperation or as painful. Love is not painful. The inability to express and share love is what is painful. "I love you so much it hurts"—you have heard this many times, and you call it love. Why does it hurt? What one is trying to describe is a confused feeling that love is need—an unfulfilled need. It would be more accurate this way: "I want you to love me so much, it hurts." Yes, that is the pain associated with love. Love itself is not painful. Love is magnificent.

Then one would ask, "Why, then, do I feel pain when I try to share myself with somebody and they reject me?" Pain comes with the inability to accept love.

"I love you."

"Why?"

"I love you."

"No you don't. You just say that."

Always doubting, always questioning a person's ability to share with you. If you can accept what I have to offer, however much love, then you have been loved and the field of energy is completed. "May I do that for you?" "Yes, if you will do it right." What does that do to the other? The transaction of love is then not completed. Pain is the result of love not being completed. How does one block this flow of energy? By refusing to receive it. It is not painful for one to love. It is painful when you do not accept love. If you block your transaction, this is painful to the potential recipient. You may not clearly understand this at this moment, but if you will evaluate what I am saying, you will find that love in itself is never painful. It is the denial of love that is painful.

At this point you may be thinking that the entities speak of love in an ideal or pure sense, much as Jesus did. This is true, and they often refer to his teachings regarding love. Is love the answer to all, as many have said?

That's a fact. Was it not Christ that said, "Love is everything"; "Love thy neighbor"? All of his teaching was based on love. As people began to accept his teaching, they began to mellow and feel tolerant toward each other, to be more forgiving of each other, to be not so critical of each other. You are only as critical of others as you are with yourself. Try it sometime. For every fault you find in your fellowman you will find it in yourself, or you will find the magnified fear of this fault in yourself. What did Jesus say to those that punished him? "Forgive them, father, they know not what they do." Do not live with an assumption that your neighbor is always knowledgeable of what he or she does.

PERSONAL LOVE AND BROTHERLY LOVE

A distinction is made between a personal, committed form of love and a broader, caring kind of love that one feels for one's neighbor or fellowman.

There are many emotional expressions of love and to various degrees. It would be easy to say, "I love you, but I am not in love with you." How is being in love different from loving? Being in love becomes a more difficult need to commit oneself to, such as to your family or to your mate. "I want to commit myself to you. I want to devote myself. With your permission, I want to share all of myself with you." I can love my neighbor because I have a desire to help him with his needs, and I share myself in proportion to that which I am capable of sharing. But I never permit myself to deplete my ability to share, because if I do, I have nothing to share.

In giving of ourselves to a friend or acquaintance in a caring or neighborly fashion we certainly will not always get a clear-cut positive response. Yet Aenka states that even in apparently one-sided love transactions a positive response may well be there even if it is not visible.

It is impossible to share yourself without their sharing themselves with you. If you respond emotionally favorably and kindly to your neighbor, they cannot help but respond favorably. I am not at this time speaking about negative people. There are some who would not respond, who would not receive your love, would not complete their aspect of the transaction. But if you do not feel inadequate in such a transaction, you would not demand something from that individual who has nothing to offer. Many people receive love but do not have the capacity to immediately initiate an act of love back to you. If you do not receive an immediate response, and if you have a string attached, it is almost impossible for that act of love to fulfill itself. Immediately, the string you have attached to your transaction begins to pull back, like a window shade.

LOVE AND COMPATIBILITY

Aenka used a simple allegory to show how one person can offer another what they can within their own limits and yet share a feeling of love and support.

It is a measure of compatibility. You see, love is a very beautiful thing. A chipmunk and a beaver loved each other very much. How could they express this love? The beaver loved the chipmunk so very much that he desired to hold, to touch, to be with. He could not do that. He was not capable of it, but he did offer the chipmunk the measure of love he was capable of offering. The only thing the beaver could offer was a ride on his tail. The chipmunk acknowledged his desire to be held and to hold the beaver, his desire to swim under the water and be with the beaver. Did these burning desires of the chipmunk cause him to retreat or withdraw the measure of love that he had to offer the beaver? He accepted his desire, and by accepting his desire he went forth and offered the beaver the only measure of love he could offer, and that was to ride on his tail. He did not allow his desires to weaken his love for the beaver. It is a very simple story of love and compatibility. (Aenka, December 1974)

DESIRE AND LOVE

There is so much to be desired. One desires many things, but
it all must be relative to compatibility. If you love somebody,
you love them with your capacity to love. Compatibility will
be the measure of love you receive in return. It is possible the
measure of love you receive in return will not fulfill all of
your desires. But what a delight to know that someone is loving you with all their capability, no matter how large or how
small! Do not confuse love with desire. Desire is always present in the human being. No one could possibly fulfill it. It is
a very motivating force, and it causes one to reach out. Let
the measure of love you receive keep the desire burning
within, so that you may be capable of giving and receiving.
Those who do not have desire and those that are not content
with a fulfillment of some of their desires give up. They
withdraw from life and from reality. Those who feel anxiety
when desire is aroused deny themselves their desires in order
to be content. That is not contentment, it is endurance. They
are so afraid of desire they run from it.

EQUALITY

*You are my brother and we are the children of one universal
holy spirit.*

Kahlil Gibran, *A Tear and a Smile*

Equality. Yes, every person has a facet of divinity, and no
one is greater or lesser than the other.

All people deserve similar respect regardless of social status,
education, abilities, or achievements. While incarnated, we as
souls are all in the same step, the same grade, and we are here for

the same reason; to complete needed experiences in the physical. That is true of all human beings, regardless of what step they are working on in the unobstructed between incarnations. The entities do not confuse the equality of man from a spiritual point of view with achievement from a physical point of view. Certainly, people deserve respect for their contributions to mankind or for their personal achievements, but this does not make them any better than anyone else.

Most people can understand this differentiation between recognition for achievement on the one hand and respect as a Facet of Divinity on the other. Some have a bit of trouble applying this attitude to recognized spiritual leaders or those who have developed considerable psychic or healing abilities. Does not the head of a church or a successful healer deserve some special place of value? Are they not "more spiritual" than we in some way?

> They are not any more spiritual than anyone else. They are simply more aware of their spiritual aspect and practice the processes; thus it appears they are more spiritual.

Again the thrust of the entities' attitude is that whereas a person deserves respect for his spiritual awareness and for the effort involved in that, his knowledge or abilities do not necessarily make him more developed spiritually than anyone else. Knowledge or abilities do not relate directly to spiritual growth in the physical. Emotional and psychological growth experiences are those primarily needed in the physical realm.

Clarification of what is often referred to as an experience of cosmic consciousness may be a helpful example concerning this basic differentiation. The phrase is used rather freely in describing spiritual enlightenment, and the experience to which it refers is held in awe by some people. Is not such an enlightened person elevated in some way? Mario responded that generally the term *cosmic consciousness* refers to a particularly strong experience in which a person is quite open to the spiritual aspect, using his or her psychic ability to tune in in a very powerful way. Other aspects of his response suggest that some who have this experience imply spiritual superiority in their descriptive sharing.

> The term *cosmic consciousness* is nothing more than a dreamed up sophisticated word to place superiority upon a natural process, to feed ego. The experience itself is simply an intuitive or psychic process that creates a vehicle for you to be in communication with other knowledge, another field of energy, such as we in the unobstructed; therefore a cosmic experience. In its natural and intended interpretation, *cosmic* simply refers to the cosmos, the universe. But what you have to understand is how often individuals brag about their orgasm; they have had the greatest.

A second dimension in which the entities view all humans as equal is that all are subject to what they call the *immutable laws*. The immutable laws, designed by the Source and operative in both the government of life and the gamble of life, are guidelines for natural living and the pursuit of one's destiny in the physical. Simply stated they are:

1. Every man is endowed with a Facet of Divinity that ensures his human dignity.
2. Each man is unique and has his individual destiny to fulfill.
3. Self-acceptance (man accepts his total personality structure —physical, emotional, intellectual, and spiritual aspects).
4. Man has the right of free choice.
5. Recompense (man accepts responsibility for his choices).
6. Independence (man bears within himself all the potential of self-fulfillment).
7. Interdependence (man accepts that he has limitations).
8. All true benefits must be earned.
9. All true benefits must be mutual.
10. Human equality (all are subject to the gamble of life and the government of life).

DESTINY

Seek, and you shall find.

—Matthew 7:7

All of us as souls are born from the Source purposefully and not in some chance manner. All souls share common destinies of general sorts, and each soul creates and pursues its unique individual destiny. The concept of destiny as presented by the entities is not drab or fatalistic (that is, passively "destined to be," with no options) but very vibrant and alive. Destiny from a spiritual point of view is charged with excitement, choice, and chance. It is an aspect of human existence that serves as a motivating and organizing force, helping us to orient our lives and behaviors toward desired goals.

The ultimate destiny of all souls is to complete their cycle of learning and return to merge with the Source. A second general destiny is the experience of rhythmic living and integrated natural behavior at some points in our incarnations. A third general destiny we all share is the necessity for experiencing at least one positive lifetime with each of our soulmates. During a physical life with a soulmate we are to experience mutual respect, benefit, enjoyment, expressions of concern or caring, support, and personal growth. We do not share a physical life with a soulmate in each incarnation.

You may have a physical destiny for a lifetime and not have it with your soulmate. You would choose another entity as a mate in that physical destiny with a specific purpose in mind.

The last general destiny shared by all souls is that of acquiring a working knowledge or skill in the three major study areas in physical life. Aenka was quick to point out that the requisite knowledge is practical comprehension and understanding, not necessarily academics or sophisticated specializations. He also pointed out that any one area of interest may well contain elements of all three general areas, even though this may not be readily apparent. As we work at gathering basic knowledge in the three general areas, we are also working on our personal choice of a major focus in one of them over our lifetimes. Once many of the basic needed experiences have been gained, "all of your other lives would have a similar orientation towards your strongest potential, whether it be art or science or religion."

From the experiences needed in the general shared destinies, each soul designs its individual destiny, its own unique stamp and configuration. Individual destinies through many lifetimes, culminating in a unique contribution to the Source, are influenced in an incredibly complex fashion by at least three major categories of factors: the unique quality of the newborn soul itself, the complicated plan prior to each incarnation referred to by the entities as the government of life, and the gamble of life.[1] While our destiny experiences in each lifetime are to be discovered and challenged by our own free choice and energy, there are spiritual/psychic resources available to us. These will be discussed in the next chapter.

CHAPTER FIVE

The Obstructed Universe: Psychic/Spiritual Influences

A still, small voice.

—1 Kings 19:12

Impingement and Intuition

With the curtain drawn, it is no easy task to identify our destiny during any one lifetime. As Mario put it one evening, "A person may develop a hobby late in life that is a crucial interest area for that particular lifetime." The Source fortunately designed a system of influences and phenomena that offers assistance in the search for individual destinies, if we can open to them. The system consists of a personal government-of-life record in the unobstructed, our guides in the unobstructed, potential to peek through the drawn curtain while incarnated, and psychic energy. The primary methods of connecting with this system are impingement and intuition. Both of these processes involve a contact between man and the unobstructed and are functions of the spiritual quadrant of our personality. In both processes psychic energy is used as the vehicle for communication.

Impingement occurs when a spiritual guide takes the initiative to impart a message to us, attempting to subtly influence a choice. Using psychic energy as a vehicle, the guide literally sends a message. We can choose to pay attention to this influence or not. Intuition uses the same vehicle of psychic energy, but the initiation of energy for contact comes from us rather than from the unobstructed.

> Impingement is when we initiate, when we impinge upon the mind. If you are projecting yourself out psychically at your initiative, and communicating with us, that is intuition. That would be a good simple description of the difference. They are essentially one and the same.

The effect of impingement or intuition on those in the body is usually experienced as a hunch, a feeling, or an urge. Occasionally there is need for a more forceful message instigated in the unobstructed, but this is not frequent.

While psychic energy facilitates transmission of the information, reception or grasping of the message is neither automatic nor easy. The message must in a very real sense get past the drawn curtain and the blocking element of the physical personality. One of the authors conceptualizes the mechanics of this process as similar to osmosis—diffusion through a permeable membrane. In a physical osmotic process, matter will pass through a permeable membrane from the direction of higher to lower pressure. With impingement the psychically or spiritually impinged energy/ information is thought of as being at a higher frequency (pressure) and our receptors for this energy at a lower frequency (pressure). Just as smoke can be blown through a paper tissue, so might this information be transmitted through our drawn curtain to conscious awareness.

After reception, there is still the difficulty of identifying the information, sorting it out from known information or random thoughts, and, it is hoped, not distorting it in translation.

There are many processes the mind goes through in an attempt to assimilate. One way is to realize that the possible foolish thought or image is new material, something your mind has not offered you through the thinking processes of learned knowledge. At other times, impingement or intuition triggers an emotional response. You have witnessed people say they have a "gut feeling" of rightness about something even though, in all practical or rational processes of the mind, they might argue that the point is ridiculous all along. But you would have an emotional feeling it is right. And then, of course, you would let nothing but fear stop you.

While most people have little trouble understanding this phenomenon, having had their own intuitive hunches or dreams, some examples will be given.

An archaeologist may search for years and be walking over his find a hundred times, or be looking in the wrong direction. All he needs is one link to add to the map or search, and so it might be impinged upon him. The scientist would snicker to himself and possibly tell his colleagues, "I have a hunch." They would follow the hunch, and it leads them to their find. . . . A person may have an out-of-body experience during sleep, and we could discuss something with them and try to keep the curtain open so it can be a meaningful dream they can remember: . . . Suppose you choose to involve yourself in a complicated mathematical equation. If it was known knowledge to a physical mind, there is a good probability your guide would not help you with it, because it would be available for your mind to be learned. You would look in your books. Now if you were having difficulty, it is possible we may impinge by in effect saying, "Go to the library" or "It would be the fifth book on the bottom row."

THE GOVERNMENT OF LIFE

*I send an angel before you to guard you on the way and to
bring you into the land which I have prepared.*
                                                    —Exodus 23:20

Our government-of-life plan, the architectural design for our
next incarnation, "is recorded and left in the unobstructed as
reference for your guides and those entities that choose to influence and impinge upon you."

It is a process associated with the archives of knowledge,
similar to the archives of knowledge but a separate division.
It is the storage of your programmed needs, desires, and experiences. No entity can choose for you, reason for you—or
make assumptions on what you need, want, or desire. But if
this information is left in the record of the government of
life, the other entities can conform to that and assist you and
other elements. You as an entity within a physical body,
limited as you are, can influence the physical mind to be
maneuvered in making decisions and experiencing such
things as you need. The government of life maneuvers you
after you have been incarnated. You have two sources of
guidance. You have your guides, all of the entities that are interested in you, and you have your own wisdom, which is
called your intuition. Intuitive guidance is not impingement
by a guide, it is your own contact with the unobstructed or
the Source. With these the government of life attempts to
maneuver you.

I will offer an example of the government of life, and you
can apply it to a million things. Say that you and your
soulmate have not had a positive experience in the physical,
and your soulmate has chosen to incarnate. In order to have
a relationship in some intimate way as mates, you would
choose to be born in the same era. Now, say your soulmate
chose to incarnate in Cambodia. In the government of life
you would record that sometime during that lifetime it would

be positive for you to meet with and mate with your soulmate, to fulfill that experience. As you program your government of life, bearing in mind your needed experiences, calculating the probabilities of chance, you notice because of the things you have experienced in your previous incarnations you would not gain the remaining elements you need if you chose Cambodia. However, there is a family in New York that will offer you experiences you need. The genetic picture is good for the personality; the environment and culture are suitable. As you grow in New York, you unconsciously find yourself as a young man having a desire or an opportunity to go to Cambodia—for school, work, vacation, whatever. Your guides will say, "Pay attention to that primitive nudging." You go, and lo and behold, who do you think you bump into. You might call this "as coincidence would have it."

You see, the government of life is like a preconscious programmed process that gently nudges you. But it can do nothing so overt as to deprive you of free choice in the body. In a similar way, the forces involved with the government of life attempt to influence the parents you choose and try to maneuver them to behave in a way that will offer you the experience and the conditioning you need to gain your destiny.

The impingement/intuitive process is not a simple or easy one. At the same time as any one individual is being subtly influenced, so are thousands of others. As Mario described various complexities, we began to understand that it is literally impossible to predict an outcome of impingement bcause there are so many factors. As Mario put it in a humorous example:

One of your guides might want to try and cause it to rain so you would miss a bus, to meet your soulmate; provided some other entity is not trying to make it not rain, so someone can catch the bus. It seems rather complicated, but it is a marvelous design.

Conflicting or competing interests within one individual and between different people are said to be under constant evaluation in the unobstructed, and decisions are based on what impingements would be most positive for all involved.

THE GAMBLE OF LIFE

A major factor complicating the government-of-life plan and influencing one's destiny is absurdly simple and yet very powerful: sheer accident. All accidents are referred to as *the gamble of life*. Large or small, they influence us in ways that will ultimately assist or interfere with completion of destiny issues during any lifetime. Physical illness, accidents, economic or political changes all affect us significantly.

Also included in the gamble of life are unpredictable changes in people with whom we have a personal relationship. Although the choice of parents-to-be is made carefully, due to their own personality or life experiences they may well change the way they relate to us after our birth, and we may thereby miss some needed experiences. War, which is never a destiny choice individually or collectively, can alter or end lives. As Mario put it, there is little to be said about these accidental events called the gamble of life. "A spider bite is a spider bite. Yes."

It is at times difficult to believe that sheer chance can have such an impact on a complex and carefully designed spiritual experience, but the gamble of life *is itself* a part of the Source's plan. It increases the challenge of life and adds the necessary factor of unpredictability to stimulate choice and sharpen problem-solving skills. It offers opportunities for learning humility and positive living in the face of possibly major disappointments.

The entities do not understate the thorns in the rose garden of life, and one of the reasons they do not become involved with predicting the future for any one person is related to these gamble-of-life issues. They are aware of many probabilities and

plans for each of us, but they cannot predict the intricate variations of chance and free-choice factors. Also, they must not be
too helpful, for we are to learn primarily on our own. If provided
silver spoons, we are not as likely to develop our own resources.
Life is essentially a high-risk, high-gain experience. While there
can be many events or people that frustrate purpose and destiny,
the ingredients needed to reach completion have been included
within each human being.

Many people say that they would like to be told clearly what
their destiny in a given lifetime is, or at least how to identify
choice based on impingement or intuition as differentiated from
psychological and personality aspects. The entities offer little
direct assistance in these areas, for the answers to such questions
are part of the reason we are here. Every individual interested in
such distinctions must evaluate and determine on his own whether
a choice to become, say, a carpenter is a destiny issue or a strictly
personal/psychological one.[1]

The entities do stress that the more we know ourselves
psychologically, the more we shall be able to differentiate our intuitive spiritual choices from psychological ones. They consistently urge personal growth and effective psychotherapy as a
means not only to reduce fear and guilt but to assist in helping
find one's own true and unique self. They also emphatically state
that a clean psychological house makes a strong foundation for
subtle tuning in to spiritual awareness.

PAST LIVES AND KARMA

For whatever a man sows, that shall he also reap . . . .
Every man shall bear his own burden.
—Galatians 6:7; 6:5

In the search for identification of purpose and destiny in this
lifetime and/or for an explanation of both misery and happiness,

some people embrace the idea of karmic consequences over lifetimes. For many, the concept of karma is what might be called a static or closed concept of destiny that allows little or no free choice. In this view, a person is seen as a victim of either circumstance or previous influence.

When this attitude is applied to the influence or effect of previous incarnations on one's current lifetime, a typical conclusion is that one is either (1) happy, healthy, wealthy, etc., as compensation for a "good" past life or reward for having endured a painful one, or (2) miserable in one way or another as a means of paying a debt for misdeeds in a past life, or as needing to experience a particular type of misery to "balance one's karma." Although there are many variations on this theme, the basic belief persists that knowledge of past lives might help one explain one's present situation and/or current life destiny.

The entities are not very optimistic about finding such connections and do not particularly encourage such a search. They teach that while we might find some consistency in our destiny over lifetimes, we are just as likely to find a different focus in each. They insist that there is no such thing as a direct carryover phenomenon from life to life. One does not accumulate karmic debts or payments over lifetimes. Karma is nothing more than consequences within a lifetime. A person might be a prominent figure in one life and nondescript in another; wealthy in one, poor in another; healthy in one, sick in another.

Past lives have little relevance to our present one other than perhaps to show us something we did not learn at those times. Aenka said that it is possible to become aware to some degree of past lives, and that such knowledge might help us "make better judgments and better choices."

Such information could govern you into behaviors and activity that should benefit you, rather than to repeat the same thing over and over again. So there is an advantage to open up these channels and gain access to knowledge available to you.

He went on to say that such peeking through the curtain was a psychic phenomenon and suggested that the ability to do this could be fostered by bringing our four personality quadrants into better harmony.

> Yes, it is a natural phenomenon that could occur quite frequently if an individual was totally accepting of his spirituality and all of the rhythmic behaviors of his psyche. You see the spiritual part of your total personality equals one-fourth.

Awareness of past lives can apparently be gained through a variety of mechanisms: dreams, visions, altered states of consciousness, intuitive thoughts or feelings, impingement. One possible method that has some current popularity is hypnotic regression, but the entities encourage much caution with this approach. The difficulty in hypnotic experiences arises in differentiating a "real" past picture from a psychologically produced "unreal" or fantasy picture. In responding to questions concerning how to make such a differentiation, the entities again direct us toward developing psychological balance. This helps minimize defensive ego needs or fears and optimizes a trust in one's own judgment. Whatever the method used, "it is all referred to as intuition, since you are initiating the contact."

> Your intuitive qualities often feed you information that can be very valuable for you, but so many times your conscious mind rejects it because it argues the point. If the intellect and emotions were functioning in harmony, your mind would consider the wisdom of the intuitive and use it.

Are there ways to help us tap our inner knowledge other than being as psychologically healthy as we can? In this day and age we hear much of spiritual attunement and methods of achieving this through such processes as introspection, meditation, or prayer. How do these fit into the spiritual scheme?

MEDITATION AND PRAYER

I shall light a candle of understanding in thine heart, which shall not be put out.
—Apocrypha, 2 Esdras 14:25

The function of meditation was described from both psychological and spiritual points of view, but the entities' primary focus is on the use of meditation as an aid to impingement and intuition.

> The convenient thing about the ritual or practice of meditation is it clears the mind of garbage and sets the conscious activity aside, whereby it is easier for one to receive impingement. That is the whole purpose of the spiritual quadrant, to tap the potential ability man has to be in touch with his spirituality. That is why introversion is a part of the whole personality—to go within.

Mario added that the meditation process, like any other procedure, can be misused.

> It is constructive in its positive form, if you are not using it to escape reality. The destructive use of it is to go into a state of meditation to avoid painful issues in living that need to be dealt with.

Aenka and Mario both speak of prayer very simply—primarily as another way to increase our contact with the unobstructed.

> What is prayer? A sincere desire when you have exhausted all of your resources and you cannot help yourself. Try it. If you have the faith of a mustard seed, you can move a mountain.

Aenka also suggested, concerning the *manner* of prayer, to "say what you feel in your heart: prayer is sometimes a confession."

The general thrust of the direction or focus of prayer is said to be best left to the individual and what he finds most meaningful. Some might find ritual prayer of a particular religion meaningful, others might feel more relevance in an individual prayer of their own devising. For those raised in the Christian church, praying to Jesus was described as quite practical and sensible. For Christians, appreciation of Jesus as a powerful spiritual figure can help focus energy, thereby increasing the spiritual connection.

> I shall say, pray to Jesus. You must realize that the river is quite wide and the water is deep. What did Christ say? "I shall be the stepping-stone to your father."

We asked Aenka to give us an example of a prayer that might be positive yet general. We were not surprised that his response was oriented towards integrating the four main aspects or quadrants of ourselves in the physical.

With the awareness of man's spiritual connections, other gifts and abilities can sometimes be recognized. Precognition, psychokinesis, psychic healing, and psychometry are some of the names applied by man to inexplicable phenomena that cannot be explained by use of our known senses. What of the energy involved here? What is the process?

PSYCHIC AND SPIRITUAL ENERGY

> *In modern quantum theory [of physics] the idea of a mathematical description of all nature has broken down. Individual quantum events . . . are not subject to any mathematic-physical law.*
>
> —Heinz Pagels, *The Cosmic Code*

There is currently a resurgence of interest in occurrences loosely characterized as psychic or spiritual phenomena. An increasing number of physical scientists are now considering the presence of fields of energy that we simply have not yet learned how to measure and which may well be related to such phenomena.[2] The many books and published research in psychic areas offer documentation supporting the existence of such unknown energy forms—so much so, in fact, that in order to ignore or deny its presence, one must be resolutely determined. Unlike many of us in the body, the entities take a very matter-of-fact attitude toward what we call psychic or spiritual experiences, including psychic healing. Once again they speak of three major forms of energy: spiritual, psychic, and physical.

Spiritual energy is referred to as being a nonphysical (as we know it) energy that operates directly from the Source. Man has no ability to harness or manipulate this energy and never will. It was not intended to be *used* by man. We can invoke spiritual energy through prayer but cannot control its appearance or its effects.

> Spiritual phenomena cannot be manipulated by the mind and cannot be controlled by the mind.

Only spiritual energy is capable of performing a miracle, which the entities define as an interference with a natural or universal law.

> A miracle can only come from the Source. We in the unobstructed can only deal with the reality that exists in the physical.

The most common example of spiritual-energy involvement would probably be a person who, according to technical medical data, "should" die but who lives and whose diseased organs suddenly manifest as perfectly whole or at least drastically improved. Anyone familiar with the Bible will recall the healings invoked by Jesus, many of which are said to have involved spiritual energy.[3]

"Evil spirits" or spiritual energy emanating from lost souls or Satan is a phenomenon that the entities are adamant in refuting. Whereas man can misuse psychic energy in some destructive ways, spiritual energy is *only* and *always* positive.

> There is no evil whatsoever in the universal energy, the spiritual energy that is the Source of all Divinity. All spiritual energy is pure. It is an all-positive energy incapable of harm.

Experiences apparently related to "evil spirits," "lower spirits," or the devil have nothing to do with spiritual energy and are the result of either psychological or psychic energy factors.

Many people become very much concerned about being "taken over" by spirits, evil or good. Such an occurrence is impossible.

> I shall remind you only one soul possesses one body, and all other spirits respect this possession. Even if the soul is experimenting with astral travel, should you leave your body for hours, another entity would not possess it because they recognize your energy pattern and have high regard and respect for your possession. You see, it is not that I could ever convince you there is no evil; I can only *communicate* to you there is no evil. The acceptance of this emotionally or psychologically can only be through reconditioning—that is, to challenge that fear and learn one can experience this and live through it.

Concern regarding one's soul being possessed is in some instances the simple result of subcultural conditioning—that is, superstitions and legends passed along through generations. In other instances such beliefs reflect a person's own repressed fears or guilts projected outside of themselves.[4] Some people learn to fear soul possession by interpreting causal connections between events that simply happen to correlate in a general time frame. However, correlation does not prove cause and effect.

Some people are fortunate enough to consciously experience or even perceive through their physical senses an entity or guide at a time of impingement. This can be startling, or frightening, and the entities offer support for those who have this experience.

What is your guide doing with you right now? He is with you during the day and while you sleep. He is always with you. There are some individuals so sensitive they can see the ethereal forms or the energy patterns. Everything the entity does in your presence is for a purpose and that purpose relates to your benefit in spiritual, psychological, and physical growth. They would not participate in anything that would not be beneficial for you.

Psychic energy is a form of physical energy man has not yet learned to scientifically detect, much less measure. Nonetheless, some people learn to manipulate psychic energy. The entities speak of this form of energy as nothing magical, although since we have not learned to detect it with instruments or control it technologically, it *seems* magical to us.

Psychic energy is a free energy. It is an independent *physical* energy provided and made available for the human species to use in a positive way. It can be used for communication; it can be used for healing.

Psychic energy is described as being distributed throughout the physical universe. Mario made a simple comparison to electrical energy and magnetic fields, both of which can be used to transmit information in addition to having their own influence and power. In helping us form a picture of psychic energy, he offered the following analogy:

In simple form, imagine the energy of the electrical current flowing through the wires in your home. You cannot see it, but it is there. The only way that form of energy can influence and cause light is through a vehicle. The vehicle is the wire. If you make the continuity or the connection, then the energy can travel to the filament. There is no escape for the energy. The energy builds up, and since the filament is weaker than the other part of the circuit, it becomes overloaded. It glows with an excess amount of energy concentrated in the weakest part of the circuit. You see, our energy is around you all the time, but there must be a vehicle to make our presence known. The vehicle is psychic energy.

Psychic energy is the energy used (with or without awareness) in tuning into what are called *psychic processes*, and its potential uses are rather staggering. In addition to its being the vehicle in making contact with the unobstructed universe, this form of free energy can be used in either passive or active/assertive modes in a wide variety of specific ways. Examples would include telepathy, clairvoyance, clairaudience, psychokinesis, and healing.[5]

What you must realize is the potential lies in every human being to understand and master these things; some master it, some do not.

Mario and Aenka emphasize that psychic energy is in itself neither good nor bad. It is simply an energy that exists and that, like any other, can be used constructively or destructively. If one is not familiar or comfortable with such energy, its occurrence can be alarming or even frightening. While rare in contemporary times, well-developed psychic abilities can be rather powerful. For example, some "apparitions" are said to be psychically produced.

Thought is a physical energy created by the mind. The vehicle for thought to travel is psychic energy. So whatever your fantasy may be, or your thoughts, the mind can use psychic energy to manifest it. It is literally possible to psychically produce a phenomenon one could see with the physical eye. However, one would have to develop psychically and achieve great powers in harnessing the energy to be able to produce that type of psychic phenomenon. It is not common.

Tales of evil supernatural forces of one sort or another have been with man for all recorded history. Such forms are not spiritual but are man-made, either by psychological self-deception or the use of psychic energy.

> The human mind was designed for the purpose of free choice, and it is potentially very powerful. Therefore a developed mind can produce in a negative way a form of energy that can harm. It is an energy produced by the physical mind, not by spiritual energy. *The only evil man deals with is in his mind.*

Knowing many people fear "black magic" types of energy, we asked Mario about potential destructive uses of psychic energy. He emphasized three points in his response: (1) it is possible to direct psychic energy for destructive purposes; (2) this can only occur if one develops great ability, which is rare; and (3) the receiver of the psychic influence has as much to do with its impact as the sender.

> There is a psychic force that can be called whatever you like to call it. A person could do you harm if he could harness enough psychic energy to influence the processes in your body. However, you are equally powerful in your energy and can block the influence that psychic energy is having on you. Beware, your own mind can become so involved with it that your own psychic energy joins that which is pursuing you and intensifies its strength. It then has the power not only to distort your mind but could disfigure you should you allow yourself to become involved with it.
>
> The greater the fear, the more imaginative the mind becomes; and these thought forms thrive on fear. The more they can frighten you, the stronger they become. Voodoo can kill you, and why does it? The individual feels the fear, feels

the pain, and the fright becomes so intense that in a sense he is frightened to death. The body chemistry literally destroys itself. Always remember negativity can never harm you by projection form if you accept its potential, if you accept the reality of it and not fear it. As I have said before, should you become aware of something of this nature about you, accept it and feel most confident in yourself. Ask it to leave and go about its business. If you do not fear it, it will dissipate. Tell it to go away, that you do not support it, and it will leave.

In responding to our concerns and fantasies about the possibility of people who might learn to use psychic energy in a powerful and destructive fashion, the entities were most reassuring when they stated matter-of-factly that this is an incredible rarity. One limiting factor is that a person intent on being destructive rather than constructive will be severely handicapped in harnessing psychic energy. His personality would need to be very much out of balance to desire destructiveness, and personality balance is required for powerful psychic development. A related question was whether or not we might initiate something destructive with psychic energy unintentionally or accidentally. The answer to this occurring to any significant degree is an unequivocable no.

In your everyday natural processes, with or without your awareness, psychic energy is used in many ways; as a vehicle for communication, for the gain of insight, for thought processes. Many of those processes occur at an unconscious level. Those things for which it is necessary to harness greater quantities of psychic energy to be used in a deliberate way with the mind are usually done in a conscious effort. No one becomes actively involved with significantly powerful destructive psychic energy except by will.

There are a few natural exceptions to this general fact (as there are to many general "laws"), one of them being poltergeist activity. This term is typically used regarding random or haphazard psychokinetic phenomena, which most often occur in the presence of an adolescent. For some reason, "the gate or valve—or whatever you would like to call it—which controls the flow of psychic energy through the brain is caused to be open."

> The adolescent, in his frustration and desperation, then takes in tremendous amounts of psychic energy and projects it out indiscriminately. He is not aware that he is doing this. But he can become aware that when he is in this state these things occur. Then it is possible for him to say "I can cause this" and then he can attempt to use this energy in destructive ways.

Such exceptions are one of the elements of the gamble of life. However, consistent with the need for a balanced personality to harness much psychic energy, an examination of recorded and observed poltergeist activity indeed shows mostly nuisance-type phenomena. Rarely has anyone been harmed.

Some participants in our darkroom sessions have had experience in other psychic studies and/or have been involved in expressive personal psychotherapy in which much "negative" energy is discharged harmlessly in an attempt to clear up unfinished emotional business. Some of these participants were concerned about the possibility of accidentally harming someone by means of psychic energy in the expresion of strong emotions in a therapeutic setting. Aenka and Mario have both said that this was not possible. They explained that motive and intent are crucially important in the release of psychic energy. Healthy expression of strong feelings with the motive of clearing oneself could not possibly cause harm to another person.

> Thought patterns are not traveling to the person you are emoting about. Your motive is to discharge and free yourself of the feelings,not with the intent or purpose to destroy or harm another human being. With that motive, the energy does not travel, it is not projected by psychic energy. The emotional energy is therapeutically and harmlessly discharged.

A number of people through the years have held a belief, or presented data, that certain geographic areas are more prone to psychic or spiritual phenomena than others. Notable among these is T. C. Lethbridge, and an excellent review of these ideas and data has been done by Colin Wilson. We asked the entities about this possibility, phrasing our questions along such lines as do such places exist, and if so, do they make psychic or spiritual connections easier for us in the physical?

There are areas in the magnetic field of the globe that can be sensed or perceived physically or psychically, but in a broad sense this is not particularly relevant. What is obvious and significant is that experiences which occur in certain localities cause them to *appear* to be high-energy places, as some of you have experienced here in this building where you meet. However, this is not primarily because any place is a special place located geographically. It is due to the unusual and high energy experiences that have been recorded or lived there, experienced there. Not only the unique experiences of the present time, but the unique experiences of those that have been associated with the place in the past. What you must remember is psychometry brings about extrapolation of events due to the imprint of experiences. Everything that you experience, every energy that is emitted in an experience, remains in that location like a fingerprint. If you are intuitive or sensitive, then you may perceive or sense what has occurred. If you are fearful without reason, you translate that perception in destructive or negative ways.

There are some parts of the globe having physical properties which add strength to these experiences. It is a physical phenomenon having to do with the energy of the Earth, the chemical composition of a particular location, and also may involve the electromagnetic properties of a particular geographic area. Such places do not create in a person a greater potential for tuning in. It is simply that energy is more available, so to speak, and in this way it may be said to be easier to tune into. Thick is thick and light is light, or thin is

thin. Can you not determine the difference? What I am referring to is the process by which you become aware of high
levels of energy. It is easier to perceive or experience.
However, I would repeat that the energy itself does not trigger, motivate, or increase one's intuitive awareness, nor does
it make you more sensitive. Because *it* is stronger, you may
be more aware of it. It is simply more obvious if you are
sensitive.

The authors had read about the idea of psychic energy lingering
in places, and we followed up with further questions about how
this actually occurs.

Impressions of the energy linger in space. How would I say
it? In all materials or the air. It is like atoms. How does your
science at this time in their development measure the age of
things? They use carbon dating for historical measures. And
what is carbon dating? Carbon dating is a process of
measurement based on atomic particles being thrown off at a
steady rate. With the samples you take you can estimate how
long ago the original sample was created because of the
depreciation or diminishing of the radiating particles. They
decrease at a relatively constant rate per year or per
thousands of years. This is a most accurate way of measuring. The same applies to an experience. It leaves energy which
permeates or impregnates a space, an area, a location. Such
is related to what you are referring to as high-energy places.
Say someone was destructively treated in this meeting
room, what you would call murder. The imprint of that experience would linger, diminishing gradually as time passed.
If you are highly sensitive and accepting, when you were in
this room you might sense or be aware of that having occurred. If you were nonfearful of your intuitive process and
your translation or interpretation is objective, then you
would perceive it in that manner. If you were fearful and
negated by attitudes about evil, then you would experience an

emotional reaction to it as something evil had happened here. That could very easily be translated incorrectly as negative spiritual energy.

If someone were looking for a house to buy and they were sensitive—in a psychic sense, to use the term loosely—they might pick up different vibrations in different houses based on what had occurred there. Say that you were out to buy a house and in your examination you walked into a bedroom. If someone had died in that bedroom and you were highly sensitive you might translate that into a negative feeling about that house *if* you had fears and unresolved feelings about death. Experience—all experience—creates an energy pattern. When you remove your physical body from the floor where you are talking to me, the outline of that experience or position will linger.

The leaving of impressions is a physical phenomenon, rather like phantom photographs. This relates in a general sense to what you call Kirlian photography. They have detected a phantom image in their electromagnetic field. The image of a missing part, such as a leaf or a finger, would be there. The physical space of the imprint lingers and denotes its existence. The electrical charge which is applied to the physical part remaining interacts with the atoms extending beyond the amputation. This occurs to a degree significant to gather or conduct the induced electrical current. Kirlian photography is measuring the electrical current, of course, not the energy of the imprint itself, because at this point it is immeasurable in your technology. But soon you may well have instruments that can measure these types of energies.

Having also heard of some recent research and data that purport to photograph nonphysical beings or tape-record nonphysical voices, we asked Mario if he could shed some light on these occurrences.

Some of these phenomena are faked, and most are artifacts. There is a possibility of obtaining either photographs or voice recordings, but it is not likely. It is more likely in photographs than in tape recordings. In tape recording the alleged voices are often created by a combination of interferences in the atmosphere combined with electrical impulses and disturbances or stray energy. When this is amplified, it appears that voice is audible. Would it be necessary for me to sit in an empty room and whisper in a tape recorder? I would much prefer you to be here. Entities usually will not attempt to communicate with incarnated beings if they are not physically present, such as in experiments in which the tape recorders are left alone in rooms. If a person is attempting to organize some means of communication and they are present, we would be likely to make an attempt to cooperate, usually within their frame of reference. If energy permitted, we would try to materialize or etherialize. It is not uncommon for someone to accidentally capture energy patterns, because we are constantly attempting to materialize, to work with the formulas that will cause it to be easier for us to communicate with you in some physical form by etherialization, materialization, or verbalization. Thus it is possible to at times obtain photographs of outlines of an entity, or to get a voice recorded on tape even without full materialization.

A significant number of people through history have reported visions or encounters of one type or another with some sort of an ethereal being. How can we discriminate between such an experience of a spiritual nature, a psychic phenomenon, and one of a self-induced or psychological nature? Aenka's response focused on the differentiation of psychic and spiritual energies.

To distinguish the difference between a psychic phenomenon and a spiritual apparition or manifestation, remember that the mind created the psychic phenomenon and can manipulate it. You can make it do what you want it to do. The mind of another person can also influence and manipulate a psychic phenomenon. If you see me materialized and sitting with you, and you could mentally or psychically manipulate me, make me disappear, cause me to respond to your command— then you would know I was psychic energy, or a manifested psychic process.

To say more about differentiation: if I am there in your vicinity and attempting to make myself known to you, I would use whatever energy possible to make my presence known. If you spoke to me, I would speak back, if it were possible. If you waved to me, I would wave back. I would try to find some means to demonstrate or show you what you are seeing. If what you were experiencing were a psychological illusion or hallucination, more than likely you could not gain a response from it. If it was psychically produced by you, you could give it direction. You could wave to it and then you could direct it or command it to wave back; but more than likely that would need to be a conscious effort to manipulate to that extent. You would usually be aware at some level of attempting that.

For another possibility, if I were an imprint of previous experience that you were psychically or intuitively tuning into, something that has been before and you were sensing the energy pattern—if you wave to it, it would not wave back. It has not substance or intelligence. Anything that has happened previously has no direction, has no intelligence and cannot repsond in the present. It is energy that exists in a form that exist*ed*. You could not change it, nor can it change itself. You cannot give it direction nor can it direct itself.

I would like to return to the distinction you are primarily interested in, which is between self-deception on a psychological basis and a true psychic or spiritual experience. It is possible you could be playing a game with yourself. You must understand the power of the mind. You could be producing a phenomenon psychically or psychologically and manipulating it without your conscious awareness. The power of the mind is unlimited in its ability to kid itself if it really wants to. So one in their research or their experience must evaluate *motive*. We have talked about motive again and

again. Literally, the mind was so designed that it could perform in power and strength almost equal to that of spiritual
energy. I would remind you that this potential is fail-safe
because there are certain universal laws and genetic laws that
psychic energy cannot violate.

VOICE CHANNELING

There is quite a history of people who have functioned as what
are generally called *voice channels* or *trance mediums*. Typically,
the person goes into an altered state of consciousness (trance) and
begins to speak. When the verbal productions are consistently
quite different from what the person usually produces in a waking
state (whether by content, knowledge, language, style, voice
quality, etc.), then the person is said to be "channeling" the information psychically or spiritually. Edgar Cayce is perhaps the
most widely known voice channel, but most public libraries have a
fair number of volumes on others as well. Jane Roberts's Seth-
material books have for some years enjoyed popularity.[6] The entities describe channeling as a simple (although not easy) process
by which a person sets aside his conscious mental activity and
allows his intuitive quadrant to "tune in" to the unobstructed.[7]
They also say that at least two frequent attitudes or beliefs held by
many channels are a bit erroneous, even though they are subjec-
tively useful. One such belief is that the channel is "controlled"
by a discarnate entity—that in a sense he is "taken over" by this
personality.[8] The other has to do with a voice change experienced
by the channel when speaking in trance.

Such beliefs are said to be either misinterpretation of the channeled information or impingement—or a belief system that the
channel finds personally supportive and thereby of assistance in
the tuning-in process. According to the entities, voice channeling
can be at most 80 percent accurate, due to the filtering factor of
the channel's personality, values, beliefs, frames of reference, etc.[9]

Responsible channels are aware of possible distortions and not surprisingly will use all procedures or attitudes they can to optimize the clarity of their reception. Should they believe, for example, that a voice change is one such criterion, they may well produce this unconsciously while in trance. The subjective experience of the phenomenon is supportive and facilitative. Such constructs or concepts are usually the result of learned attitudes. Some voice channels believe that their voice needs to change in order to channel at all. As such, the voice change is a ritualistic act that is in fact supportive of the person's ability and thus assists in tuning in.

It is another voice that they construct. There is no such thing as possession.

In a sense, such alterations are necessary if we *believe* them to be —otherwise, not.

PRECOGNITION AND OTHER POSSIBILITIES

The entities hold a dim view of using psychic energy in precognitive or predictive processes unless they serve some important purpose, such as saving a life. In general, future-tellings are described as extrapolations (whether by observable or psychic methods) from known factors and sets of probabilities and possibilities, any one of which may come to pass if other things happen that are themselves contingent possibilities.[10]

Instead of focusing on such probability estimates (particularly if one is arrogant enough to assume that a probability is a certainty), Mario and Aenka encouraged developing our psychic abilities for enhancing intuition and impingement, spiritual awareness and growth, and in positive behaviors of a variety of types. They decry the use of psychic energy for ego purposes.

Many people, missing a feeling of contact with a loved one now deceased, naturally wonder or ask about the possibility of getting in touch with the discarnate soul. Mario's response to these inquiries suggests that sending messages to the soul of a departed loved one is a very positive use of psychic energy, but he is pessimistic regarding getting any response.

> If there is someone with whom you have been very close or have loved, and you want to communicate to them, all you need to do is to think or say whatever you choose. They will be aware of your thoughts. It depends on your motive for wanting to make contact.

He added that any attempts in the unobstructed to return a response would be evaluated from the point of view of what might be the most positive for the incarnated individual's growth and destiny during this lifetime.

The entities speak easily of the potential use by man of psychic energy: more sensitive intuition, more openness to impingement by guides, increased awareness of our spiritual aspect and the awesomeness of the universe, healing—the list is long. One possibilty among many is an increased communication/communion of some type directly with the archives of knowledge.

> Man is capable, without even contacting us, to do this. You are this very moment capable of opening your mind to this knowledge.

OUT-OF-BODY EXPERIENCES

For the things which are seen are temporal, but the things which are not seen are eternal.
—2 Corinthians 4:18

Even though our body and soul are tightly intertwined and the curtain is drawn during our incarnation, the entity within us has "out-of-body" experiences (OBEs) all through our physical life. When the entities speak of OBEs, they are referring to our spiritual essence literally leaving the physical body and traveling either in the obstructed or to the unobstructed, where we may communicate with our friends as energy patterns. During an OBE, the soul usually first assumes an ethereal form resembling our physical form. If the OBE is limited to mostly temporal traveling in the obstructed universe, it will probably stay in this form. If the entity wishes to make more direct contact with the unobstructed, it may or may not change from this ethereal shape to its original energy pattern. We are not usually aware of leaving our body, as this occurs most naturally in sleep, when the physical body is at rest and safe. We do not usually have a clear memory of the OBE since the memory is effectively screened from our conscious mind on return to the body. This is so designed in order to maximize the challenges during the search for individual destiny. It does happen occasionally that some memory fragments remain with us upon our return to the physical world.

OBEs are said to be not only natural, but needed.

> It is like a nurturing. You could not survive adequately unless you left your body and visited home, which is the unobstructed universe. It nurtures you because you are a prisoner in that physical body. During your sleep, the natural process was provided that you have the opportunity to leave your body. To your conscious mind it is nothing more physical than experiencing sleep.

Mario again emphasized the importance of separating, in our thinking, the soul within from the physical body when he stated:

> You in this physical body have all the awareness that I do in the unobstructed. It is just that as a prisoner in there, you are not conscious of this. That is why it is designed in a natural way, without learned techniques, to leave it at will.

Regardless of our destination during an OBE, the experience is described as always a positive and even exhilirating one for the soul. This information appears to be in contrast with some of the descriptions given by Monroe, Fox, and others of unpleasant and even frightening experiences.[11] When we asked about such nightmarish aspects, Mario responded that such experiences were not those of the soul but of the physical personality as it struggled with attempts consciously to integrate memory fragments of an OBE in the context of personal psychological factors or culturally conditioned fears.

> In astral travel in a well body it is easy to experience apprehension, but it is not the entity within you that is experiencing this. It is the physical body that is experiencing this, the alertness of the physical survival drive. Once you can alleviate this problem, you can freely become acquainted with astral travel. Once you can leave your body, go to another room, or feel free to travel, then you are completely aware of entities about you. Their energy patterns will be in form or shape similar to your physical body. At death there is no fear because the body is not in a state to experience these sensations.

Some people learn to have OBEs volitionally, but Mario emphasized that frequency of OBEs should be a function of need rather than overindulgence.

> One point I must make is, yes, it would be nice to think you have the freedom to leave your body anytime you want to. When your environment is painful, then you could escape and leave your body. But you must understand the responsibility you have and the spiritual eagerness to gather physical experiences. Say that you left your body at this particular moment and your body experienced something. If you are not in it, then that experience means nothing to you. Do you understand what I mean? So the entity within usually does

not choose to leave your body when you have an opportunity to experience something in the physical, because you are here to gather those experiences. While your body is that of an infant, you leave the body many times during sleep for contact and nurturing, but not as often as you may think. When you claim the body, you are very proud of it and you want to become familiar with it. You want to be in there, to have all the experiences that the infant is exposed to.

Aenka attempted to explain the mechanics of OBEs.

You can call it either astral projection, astral travel, or out-of-body experiences. It involves an energy field, an energy force that must be exact in size and quantity. It must be stable enough to keep the energy within its own pattern, to maintain a stability sufficient to keep the physical body molecularly sound. When the proper vibration is reached, one can project himself from the physical body. You would never astral-project yourself without the energy being perfectly coordinated. It need be said should the body be awakened before the energy reenters, although it is *highly* unlikely this would ever occur, some physical damage might occur. One might equate it to a "rude awakening."

According to Mario, the Source designed a fail-safe factor into the phenomenon of OBEs. It is *impossible* for a soul not to return to the body immediately if there is any significant physical threat to the body.

This is the *silver cord* you have heard psychics speak about. The silver cord always ties you to your body. It is an imaginary cord, of course, but it is an energy permanence. You would not leave your body unless this energy was so designed and so perfect there would be no concern about what happens to your body. With astral projection or astral travel, you leave your body and take a trip to the moon. While you are having a glorious time with your energy pattern observing the moon, your physical body is comfortable and out of danger. Suddenly the gamble of life threatens your body without warning—a bolt of lightning, an earthquake, an aircraft plunging into your home—any of the things due to the gamble of life that you are subjected to. You must be back in that body before it is struck dead. That is the reason for all of these factors to be perfectly in harmony.

Fears of not returning to the body or dying while out of body are unfounded. There are no lost or trapped souls.

Those feelings are psychological. It is fear only, earthly fear and physical fear.

While there is no danger of being separated or lost from the body during an OBE, there is potential danger to the physical body or personality if we stay out of the body too much or too long in a willful manner.

For one reason, if you stay away from the body more than the required period of time, a physical body will become disoriented and possibly dysfunctional or dis-eased. The body might become neurologically disarranged, and the physical then would not function in a capacity of reason and rationale. So it is vitally important that the exercise of out-of-body experience is not abused. Man has the capacity of choice if they learn how to leave their body on command, even in a waking state. But it is far safer to allow that process to occur in a natural setting—that is, when the body is at deep rest or sleep.

Now curiosities naturally must be satisfied. If one were using out-of-body experiences in a research process or in an attempt to gain information, to explore the universe, it would not be safe to do it for long periods every day. It is also true, when you learn to astral travel and you do it in a controlled or deliberate process, those experiences would be applied to the natural process. By this I mean you would not likely have an out-of-body experience when the body is in deep rest. There would be an exchange which serves as a safety process. With man's right of free choice, he could definitely abuse his body and mind seriously if he indulged in astral travel excessively. He would find himself becoming disoriented and dissociated from the physical. Soon he would be staying out of his body more than he was in it, and he would lose all reason. I realize this may sound like spirit does not have the intelligence to maintain its rightful place, but souls cannot violate choice of the physical personality or change characteristics of a physical body. They must accept a body and they are subject to the principles rightfully given the body and the mind, including the right of choice. If the body abuses itself to where it is difficult for the entity to stay in it, the entity cannot violate genetic code and restore the body.

The OBE is different from psychedelic or psychological experiences and should not be considered as the same. One evening a participant was asking questions about what she believed to be OBEs while she was on LSD. Aenka responded,

I shall tell you, you were not astral traveling. You were hallucinating, a strictly mental process. Under the influences of drugs, your Facet of Divinity would not leave the body spiritually. Psychologically and mentally you may feel or see things, but it is an hallucination, a trick of the mind. Your mind is capable of producing so many phenomena.

While usually we have no clearly conscious, complete memories of our OBE experiences, it appears possible that we can increase our capacity for such remembering.

When you go out and come back, we refer to it as the curtain being drawn. Usually none or very little of that experience is recorded in your physical mind—the memory bank, the nervous system. Occasionally there is a crack left open, the imprint of some of that energy having come back with you and not erased. So therefore it leaves its imprint upon the physical mind, and upon awakening you can remember it like a dream. If you practice, you can even keep the curtain open and bring back much information or experiences after your visits. You can learn to pass that experience on to your physical mind.

Jay Barham, Marti's husband and a minister, has been involved in psychic and spiritual studies for many years and has been the most consistently reliable channel in our darkroom experiments. He has had a number of memories of OBEs, and some quotations from one of his seminar presentations will be offered here as an example of human attempts to describe the experience of being in the unobstructed.

"If you have a true out-of-body experience of the unobstructed universe, it is impossible for it to be negative. The unobstructed is beautiful. Our physical substance cannot tolerate the energy, the brilliance of light and energy you can experience there. That is one of the reasons the curtain is drawn. Only in an out-of-body experience, when you are still connected to the physical by the silver cord, can you tolerate or experience fully the impact of the unobstructed. When you are there, you can experience entities in their natural form, each with their own identity. Entities there do not have a physical shape, they have an energy pattern. There are millions of them. They do not communicate verbally; it is more like a thought communication, an awareness. You don't see them physically, but you experience them in four dimensions.

In the unobstructed you see colors you cannot describe in physical terms. You experience every molecule, the total essence of energy. It is nothing but ecstasy. It really *is* similar to physical orgasm multiplied. In the physical we can only tolerate and absorb the pleasure of orgasm for a limited time, that is why it is limited. And that is why in the unobstructed you have to be separated from the physical, to be able to absorb the ecstasy. I wouldn't really recommend out-of-body experiences to a cosmic-type level. It is nice to be able to validate some of your learning processes, but if you have truly been through the tunnel and in that light, it is not easy to orient yourself back here.''

Jay at one time requested "to go to the limit of the unobstructed to experience the threshold of the three universes. I asked if it were possible to enter the Source's universe to gain firsthand information about it. I was flatly refused and was told it would be a total violation of a universal law, that no entity born from the Source can enter that Source until they have finished their lessons. I was allowed to go to the threshold and did gain permission to experience or communicate with an entity that had merged with the Source. It was maybe like visiting someone at a borderline where you talk with them through a glass wall. I did this and never want to do it again. Such experiences are so overwhelming that, by comparison, physical life can become dull and monotonous.''

One night in a darkroom session an entity spoke of Jay's experience.

He was taken to the chambers, so called, to the "twilight zone." He was given a glimpse, through a window, of the beauty and power it contains.

Access to our psychic avenue and thereby to a variety of types of spiritual contact as discussed in this chapter is described as simple but never easy. The curtain is drawn and there is enormous clouding, interference, blocking, and distorting caused by cultural conditioning and our own personal emotional distortions. Fear, guilt, ego trips, greed, power, manipulation—all interfere with clear intuition and nondistorted use of psychic abilities.

True humility and love are requisites for appropriate optimal use of our psychic abilities and contact with the inner soul, and the entities encourage much self-study and emotional growth work in or outside of formal psychotherapy to help build a strong foundation. For those interested and willing to undertake much experimenting—and take some lumps along the way—the possibilities are apparently almost infinite. And, without a doubt, such opening up assists greatly in our quest for completion of destiny and return to God.

CHAPTER SIX

Look Homeward, Angel

O death, where is thy sting? O grave, where is thy victory?
—1 Corinthians 15:55, King James Version

DEATH

Life for a soul is endless in a very real sense. Even before we are born as entities we live in some fashion as a tiny part of the Source. In being born into the unobstructed we as souls are given a significant measure of separation from the Source and a unique identity. Each of us builds upon, modifies, and amplifies this identity as we challenge experiences in the body and our tasks in the unobstructed. Life as a Facet of Divinity is continuous, and what appear to be stopping-places are in fact stepping-stones as we continue our journey from and to the Source.

Death as a reality exists only for the physical body and the physical personality of that body. To say that the soul lives on after physical death is not an attempt to deny the emotional and psychological realities of a person's reactions to death. The experience of loss and subsequent grief are quite real and are themselves part of the human experience that we must go through and learn to handle.[1] Recently the natural psychological processes of death, dying, and grief reactions have begun to be explored systematically, and a number of books have appeared on these subjects.[2] It is not the psychological aspects of death that we wish to address here, but the physical and spiritual aspects of death from the viewpoint of our soul.

The entities consistently speak of physical death as being much misunderstood.

I would much prefer to talk about the positive aspects of dying in the natural process in an attempt to eliminate the fear of death, because essentially there is no death to life. Life is constant. There is no end to it, but there is an end to physical life. The physical body is designed to live and respond for a reasonable number of your years to offer you the opportunity to gain those physical and psychological experiences which you choose. Providing the gamble of life will be kind to you, the physical body will live, as has been said, three-score and ten—about sixty-five or seventy years. That does not mean it could not deteriorate sooner or that it could not live a great deal longer. It means there is a reasonable length of time alloted. If you love your body and are kind to it, help it through the exposure to atmosphere and environment, it will serve you well.

The death of the body is inevitable. It is designed for a natural procedure of development, and it continues to grow until it reaches its maximum development. Then it begins to deteriorate. There is no thing or no one that can interfere with this natural deterioration. It is inevitable. You can alter it somewhat scientifically, but you cannot interfere permanently. To change it significantly would be interfering with the universal laws. Should you attempt to alter the body to any great extent, serious mutation would develop and it would be . . . the end of physical life as it was intended.

Death itself is said to be painless, whether it occurs abruptly or at the end of a lingering illness.

Many people believe there is pain in death. There is no pain to death. The physical body only experiences pain prior to shock.

This statement should not be interpreted to mean that we experience no pain *prior* to death, for the dying process may indeed be painful. However, a significant amount of that pain which may be experienced prior to death, especially in a lingering illness, is said to be self-induced, due to fear and other emotional attitudes. Acceptance of approaching death apparently can have much to do with lessening of pain.

The more emotionally accepting a person is of death, the less pain. In those circumstances where severe physical pain itself is experienced without psychological augmentation, the Source designed built-in safeguards that limit the sensation of conscious pain. Beyond a certain level of pain there is no pain sensation, even though the body may appear to be suffering considerably. An example of this would be cases of severe physical trauma.

The mechanisms responsible for absence of pain during the death experience itself are said to differ depending upon whether the death is (1) lingering, (2) relatively quick, or (3) sudden. The common factor in all of these is that prior to the irreversible separation of the entity within from the physical body, the entity within protects us in one way or another.

For those who experience a lingering death, OBEs often increase. These serve as a second pain-limit function, for when we are out of the body it is impossible to experience pain. In addition, the OBEs assist us in preparation for our transition back to the unobstructed.

When there is a lingering death where you are dying from natural decay or from some terminal disease, many days before death occurs the body ceases to sense pain. With acceptance and positive submission, there is a sense of relief and comfort about the body. A few days before death, the entity within also begins to be more free to come and go, to leave the body, to astral travel and come back to the body. This helps with the acceptance of death. At times you can actually remember this and associate with it.

Many people have commented on psychological transformations in some dying persons, a light in their eyes, a feeling of peace near physical death. OBEs can help facilitate these experiences.

OBEs related to what are called near-death experiences (people who were clinically very near death but were revived) have been studied by a number of researchers, one of the most important of whom is Michael Sabom. In his cleanly prepared research and clearly written book are many documented OBEs that were experienced as transcendental and literally life-altering in regard to attitude towards death and life after death.[3] While a person's individual frame of psychological reference affects such an experience, in a "typical" near-death experience, Mario says, "euphoria would be the word."

You find many individuals that scientifically have been brought back to life in your surgeries or after cardiac arrest. The person's body was so close to death that the euphoria was experienced. Sometimes the medical patient becomes angry at the physician for bringing him back to physical reality.

While OBEs near death (in either lingering illness or a near-death experience) can be very reassuring of continued life, even then we get only a glimpse of our true spiritual essence. Our awareness is still limited.

You will have immediate awareness of the unobstructed, because the entities there must respect your efforts and your desires to leave your body in astral travel. However, those entities would stand back until you are free from your body and only then would they move in and let their presence be known. They must be sure you do have this desire to leave your body, and it is only with this knowledge they can join you. This is why when you astral travel you do not immediately recognize the energy patterns of the entities in the unobstructed.

Another factor that prevents us from a full merging in the unobstructed prior to physical death is the silver cord.

Another reason that you do not immediately recognize energy patterns of entities is the lifeline called the silver cord. It is a form of energy or awareness such that you cannot leave your body permanently before physical death. You are always in contact with your physical body. It is impossible to leave the body and forget it. You must come back in astral travel. There is no way you can leave it and stay away from it. That is one of the laws of nature that govern it, otherwise you would not be permitted to leave it. You must be in your body when it dies. So if you were out of your body, you would know it was about to die, what moment. You would immediately reenter it. There would be no way you could avoid it. It is impossible.

Where there is awareness of impending death even in a relatively quick death, such as by drowning, fire, or from a fall, the entities say that there is still an adequate time of preparation both for the avoidance of pain and the beginning of the transition. One aspect of this is going into a state of physical shock triggered by emotional fear, both of which serve to numb the body from pain.

It is the fear or the shock the body goes into. For example, an individual is pushed or falls out of a window or off of something very high where their life is in imminent danger.

When the physical body is confronted with danger, severe danger, it will go into shock, and the natural fear causes this.

A second process in a quick death that helps us move towards the transition is a review of one's life as in a time-altered state, a process that somehow results in a feeling of detachment and tranquility. Although the entities say that this process can occur in any type of death other than sudden, they seem to emphasize its importance in a quick death.

In anything except sudden death, there is a stage within which you prepare the body. In an individual who falls, before he hits and the body dies, the mind goes through a slow-motion process of reliving his life.[4] The sensation of tranquility prior to impact will be experienced.

In sudden death, different mechanisms are at work to prepare us for the transition. By sudden is meant immediate, as in being killed instantaneously by a bullet or a blow to the head with no awareness that one is dying.

In sudden or instant death there would be no opportunity for preparation. You do not need preparation, because you would have no physical awareness of the loss of your life or of pain and thus no need for assistance with your emotions.

Regardless of the type of death or the rate of the death process, the entities focused again and again on death as a *spiritual* event as well as a physical event. The preparation processes we have been discussing are intended to aid our *physical* personality in accepting a transition that is to occur: the separation of the soul within from its physical carrier.

In responding to our many questions about death and the relative roles of the soul and the physical personality, the entities would often follow their responses by returning to the purpose of a soul's being in a body and the laws by which it operates in leaving the body. They emphasized that regardless of the physical or emotional condition of the physical body and personality, the entity would not and could not leave permanently prior to death. The purpose of being in the body is to acquire experiences and learn from them, regardless of the circumstances. But could not an entity who is still with the physical body have a *desire* for the body to die?

As an entity you have no say. The only thing you, as an entity, can do is stay with the physical body till it dies. In the case of coma, extreme pain, or lingering illness, the entity has the freedom to leave, to come and go. But you cannot leave it permanently until it dies.

We asked if this applied even in situations where a person was being kept alive by life-support equipment without which he would die.

The entity will not leave the physical body until it dies. The entity neither encourages nor discourages since there is total understanding of what is occurring. Even if they kept this physical body alive for fifty years, the entity would still stay with the body until it died.

Concerning the use or nonuse of life-support machines with a comatose person and the ethics or values involved, Mario made a number of comments.

These are very serious decisions, for emotional or psychological traumas can occur within the physical body. The entity is totally aware of this and would continue to stay with the physical body so long as it was alive, even if a person were being kept alive against their wishes. The entity within will not interfere with choices that are being made regarding physical life-support. This is all generally a part of the government of life and the gamble of life and are issues only for those physical personalities involved.

When all parts, all primary functions of the physical body, cease, it is dead.

Is the definition of brain death, then, accurate?

I will say your scientists have very well calculated the possibilities. They are very accurate in their assumption that when this occurs, the physical body will soon follow. There is no chance of its ever recovering. For all practical purposes, as far as science is concerned, the body has ceased to live. It would not offend the entity to take whatever action you would like to take. The controversy with this is nothing more than what is a child and what is not. It is fear that alarms the attending individuals. It is not their fear for that entity, it is their fear of themselves being in the same position.

Regarding awareness of the moment of death itself, "it is like preparing your body for sleep."

In going to sleep, you become very comfortable with yourself. You are not conscious or aware of when you go to sleep. You lose consciousness. This is the way death is. There is an end to your physicalness, and then occurs the entity-awareness that your body is dead. Then you begin your transition back to the unobstructed.

TRANSITION

Behold, I tell you a mystery: we shall not all die, but we shall all be changed.
—1 Corinthians 15:51

Once a physical body loses its consciousness in death and you leave it, you have an awareness as the entity you are, not as a physical experience. You do not experience the transfer physically in your mind. The consciousness changes from physical to spiritual awareness and reference points.[5] You cannot compare the awareness as an entity with the senses of your physical body. The entity that you are is completely aware of leaving your body, and once you leave it, you can look at it and observe it just as I look at you and observe you.

The transition of the soul after physical death, from being at home in the body to being at home in the unobstructed, is a gradual one. It takes from several hours to several days to feel fully acclimated back in the unobstructed, and there are three phases of the process. While some people construe this acclimatization as confusion, the entities stress more that it is a period of refamiliarization after being so intimately involved with a physical body and personality.

The first stage of separation is referred to as the etherealization stage. During this time, the spiritual energy that constitutes the soul is released from the body but is still tied to it by psychic energy. This psychic energy enables the entity to assume an ethereal physical form resembling, or identical to, the physical body we have just left.

The shape of your energy pattern when you leave your body is very much in the form of your physical structure. It will maintain that shape in an ethereal form, a total energy form that is usually invisible.

The time for this stage can be seconds to hours, and the duration is said to depend in part on an individual's need for experience in this stage. This is the stage wherein we are greeted by the souls of our deceased loved ones, who assume an ethereal shape for the purpose of helping us feel comfortable and reconnected more quickly. In this stage some or all of our spiritual guides will also take on an ethereal form and "introduce" themselves to us.[6] The guides help prepare us for the next stage, which is the transition to a pure energy form.

In a sense, the contacts just mentioned reaffirm connections both to the physical life that we have just left and the continuity of life after physical death. Although such contacts are not absolutely necessary, they are facilitating and supportive; they literally give our energy a boost for further transition. Mario compares the meetings and greetings to a child coming home after school. While the child can care for himself in the familiar home, the presence of a parent and /or siblings adds warmth and nurturing to his homecoming.

It is interesting to note that the ethereal physical form is usually anatomically "perfect." This is said to explain why some people with damaged bodies report after a near-death experience that they were able to sing, dance, see, and the like. This perfect-body aspect is explained as simply a part of the Source's design to enhance the beauty of the transition and prepare one for rebirth into the unobstructed as an energy pattern.

Depending on a variety of factors, it is possible that "sometimes up to three days you will be in the ethereal physical form."

This is one reason so many physical beings have made stories about ghosts. Some people are very sensitive to these energy patterns or even a less condensed pattern of energy than that of etherealization. They have observed the experimentation with etherealization of spirit leaving the body or near the body after death. Etherealization is only an energy form dense enough that the physical eye can see. When detected by the physical eye, you can see through it. It would be like looking through glass, but you could still see the outline. Prior to this, often there are collections of ectolasm which take on the effect of smoke or clouds or fog. It is very moist, and it feels almost like jelly. That is why many individuals who have experienced the touch of ectoplasm find their hands moist, like hand cream. In materialization, somewhat the reversal of this procedure is taken—that is, going from ethereal to ectoplasm and on into solidification of solid form.

After the initial "celebration" and orientation in ethereal form, we are ready for stage two. This consists of a shift in energy form from physical shape to "the natural form of the pattern of energy you are in the unobstructed." With this shift we are at first bound to psychic energy, one reason for which is to buffer the enormous sense of beauty and expanded awareness that we experience immediately upon assuming our pure unobstructed forms.

Even with psychic energy as a buffer, the transformation is said to be literally indescribable, perhaps not dissimilar to the birth of an infant suddenly assailed by sights, sounds, touch, smell, etc., of the physical world after the relative quietness of the womb. In much the same way we, as pure energy forms, are assailed by an enormously expanded system of stimuli and experiences. Some of our friends who met us in the ethereal stage stand by once again to aid in the transformation, this time in their pure-energy forms.

After the relatively brief second stage, we enter the third. The transition to this stage consists simply of severing the silver cord—that is breaking our connection to psychic energy. We are now fully back in the unobstructed and ready to begin our task there.

After a period of adjustment or orientation, you begin your evaluation of the physical-life experiences you have just completed. You correlate that with your complete knowledge of all the other experiences you have had throughout all your incarnations, knowledge you are not aware of while you are in the physical. You evaluate these experiences to determine whether or not there are others needed to complete your physical destiny. If there are other experiences you feel necessary, you will choose to return. You are the sole judge of your growth. No other entity, no other source of energy, judges you. Other entities are about you, but they do not assist because you are as knowledgeable of your growth as they are. They would have no criticisms or judgments to make about your growth. The guides only assist you in the physical in attempts to impinge those truths which would guide you while you are in the physical. If you have completed your physical destiny, you are then ready for concentrated studies in the unobstructed and merging with the Source.

MERGING WITH THE SOURCE

When we have finished our learning in the physical and our tasks in the unobstructed, we are ready to merge with God. We finally go home to become a directly contributing part of the unfathomable Source of all there is. When ready to merge with the Source, "you experience a transformation in your energy pattern in the unobstructed, allowing you to penetrate the invisible barrier of the Source."

For all practical purposes, you then become one with the Source and other souls, even though you retain your unique identity. You communicate within the Source as each cell of your body communicates one with the other. There is no loss of identity, just as there is not a loss of identity of any one grain of sand on your beaches. To you, a beach may be just sand you walk upon. But each grain is separate and has its own identity. Within the Source, it is the combined power of individual Facets of Divinity that make up the Source of Divinity.

Many prophets and wise men have closely identified through impingement the process of merging with the Source. This has been translated as heaven. What they are trying to identify or spell out is the heavenly body which is the height of ecstasy or pleasure, completion. There is an ecstatic celebration for this rebirth back into the Source. It is very difficult to describe in a manner which the physical mind can comprehend, and I do not say this to intimidate anyone or to challenge their capabilities. It is similar to the exhilaration one experiences on reentering the body after astral travel. If you multiplied by a thousand times the most widely

known maximum pleasure that the physical body can experience, what you call orgasm or climax, you would be
close. With each mergence cycle there is great celebration involving many entities and many energies. Some in the
physical tune in psychically or intuitively to these types of
energies. In fact, some of your symphonic music has been
stimulated from this transformation process.

It is difficult at times for an individual to understand the
purpose of the evolutionary process from the Source and
back to the Source. Why do we accumulate our knowledge?
The very purpose is the expanded growth and knowledge that
is returned to the Source. With the birth of new entities and
eventual mergence with the Source there is a continual adding
to the Source's strength, knowledge, and power. So the
Source itself continues to grow. That is why the aspects of
reincarnation and evolution were designed. As evolution continues, the Source becomes greater, stronger, and there is no
limitation to the expansion. You have gone to the moon in
your lifetime. A thousand years from now you will be traveling to other galaxies. It all has to do with progress, evolutionary studies, and the progress of the universe.[7]

CHAPTER SEVEN
Authors' Postscript

While we all share the ultimate destiny described in this book, each of us has his or her unique destiny on the journey home. We are each truly one of a kind, as are our fingerprints. It is our challenge to enhance our uniqueness during many lifetimes. This necessary task can be very frustrating. Yet only when this process is complete can we contribute to the Source and in our small way share that glory and that responsibility.

The meaning of individual destiny during a lifetime often perplexes us while we are mortal. As we mature during physical life, our private thoughts go increasingly in the direction of meaning and purpose to our life. Am I on my destiny track this lifetime? Have I chosen the right career? Am I violating personal values for success in work? Do I give enough to my loved ones and society, or do I take more than I give? What is my purpose in life? Am I satisfying my own personal growth needs as a human being even though I may be fair and loving to others? These are not easy questions, nor are they intended to be. The challenge of life is enormous, the task arduous. We cycle through pleasure and pain, certainty and doubt, nourishment and starvation. We soar with satisfaction, sink in despair.

When people sincerely reflect on the direction and quality of their life, they often feel confused or miserable. Our contemporary society overwhelms us with superficial misdirection and destructive influences. We are often taught, directly and indirectly, to measure success in life not by personal meaning and satisfaction but by money, power, and images. Growing up in such a culture, with perhaps personal fears and guilts added by well-meaning but distorted parental influence, our task of finding inner meaning is made incredibly difficult. Much time and energy that could be used more constructively is channeled into worry. Our learned competitiveness and harsh self-assessment often cheat us from experiencing feelings of success and genuine pride in facing challenges and dealing with responsibilities.

The authors of this book are no different from you, the reader. We share the same humanity and struggle in our lives as everyone else. We readily accept the threads of destiny as woven into the fabric of the humanities. As professional psychologists, ours is a unique privilege of touching the lives of others as counselors, teachers, and friends. The complexity of man and the interrelationship of our physical/emotional/intellectual/spiritual components are concepts readily accepted by us and many others in the field of psychology. This holistic approach prompts us to try to integrate these teachings into our individual professional practices. We feel that this attempted integration enhances our clinical effectiveness without interfering in any client's personal belief system.

We consider ourselves very fortunate to have been exposed to the teachings set forth in this book. Putting what we consider spiritual truth into words is satisfying, but meaningful only to the extent that the words are of some assistance to ourselves and others who share a search for God. It is not important whether you agree with our beliefs. Underneath our conscious egos, we *all* know spiritual truth. What is most important is to appreciate our own inner wisdom and to work at opening ourselves to it. Our souls wait patiently for us to connect more solidly.

It is nearly impossible for any individual not to feel forlorn and lost from time to time. Let us not be dismayed. The Source's plan is fail-safe. Outer influences as well as inner psychological forces may to some degree alter our pursuits, but nothing and no one can stop our growth and ultimate destiny. As Mario puts it:

There is no way you cannot get home.

NOTES

INTRODUCTION

1. Aries, Phillippe, *The Hour of Our Death*. A remarkably thorough and well-referenced history of attitudes/beliefs about death over many centuries. The author states, "Until the age of scientific progress human beings accepted the idea of a continued existence after death. One finds evidence of this belief in the first tombs of the middle Paleolithic period with burial offerings" (p. 95).

2. Lorimer, David, *Survival? Body, Mind and Death in the Light of Psychic Experience*. A well-researched and very readable summary of theories and attitudes about life after death, or lack of it, covering centuries and discussed from many points of view.

3. Gallup, George, Jr., and Proctor, William, *Adventures in Immortality*. From the jacket of this very readable book, which is essentially a description of a contemporary nationwide survey on beliefs/attitudes towards the possibility of an afterlife and the near-death experience, comes the simple statement that "A full two-thirds of all Americans believe in life after death." This book also gives some examples and many statistics attesting to the universality of the near-death experience and its typical effect on the experiencer.

Moody, Raymond, *Life After Life*. Anecdotal accounts of persons describing the near-death experience and its effect on their lifestyle, beliefs, and values, as presented by a physician-philosopher. While sharply criticized by the scientific community for poor methodology, this book had tremendous impact on the general American public.

4. Sabom, Michael, *Recollections of Death: A Medical Investigation*. A rigorous investigation of the near-death experience by a cardiologist who self-admittedly thought he would "disprove" Moody's anecdotal data. As a result of his tightly controlled study, he was forced to change his personal attitudes and to honestly challenge his own personal beliefs. "Over the centuries, a variety of experiences have been recounted by people who have almost died. A brilliant light, a beautiful landscape, the spirits of long-departed loved ones, all have figured in what were referred to as visions of death. . . . Now more than ever before, people are returning from the threshold of death. Because of recent advances in

medical technology hearts can be restarted, breathing restored, blood pressure sustained. Patients who in the not so distant past would surely have died are now being brought back to continue their earthly existence. They are remembering more of their experiences, and we are listening" (p. 1).

Ring, Kenneth, *Life at Death*. In sequential researches this psychologist is attempting to further differentiate types and aspects of psychological functioning as they relate to differences in individual near-death experiences. He has also been the driving force behind the International Association of Near Death Studies, an excellent source of reference material for this phenomenon (IANDS, Box U–20, University of Connecticut, Storrs, CT 08268).

5. Sabom, *Recollections of Death*, p. 152.

6. Sabom, *Recollections of Death*, p. 152.

Regarding the contemporary attitude of man looking to science to "explain" the universe and universal questions, Arthur Young in *The Reflexive Universe* makes a cogent statement: "[Man] has for millions of years depended on something higher, on something beyond himself and suddenly he tries to cut this off. He cannot so easily change himself. So what results? As he has banished his worship from consciousness, it seizes control through his subconscious. He worships a science. This is the most absurd distortion, that man with all his foibles, has ever indulged. For science is a tool. It provides the means for effecting his will. It should not be worshipped because its nature is service. We may not ask of science whether man has a will of his own because science is committed to the doctrine that the uncertainty which would occur if a machine had a will of its own must be eliminated. If the battery says 'no' when we want it to start the car, we get a new battery. No tool would be any use if it had a will of its own. A tool is a means used by our will. So it is absurd to turn to the exponents of means, who are expert at removing self-determination from mechanisms, for any illumination of that aspect of experience which they have been at pains to eliminate. But we cannot answer that need of man by telling him not to consult science. He is so constituted that he must have advice. He depends on something higher than himself. If it is taken away from him, he invents it; he constructs it out of the materials at hand. In an age when religion falters, he makes a cult of computers. . . . he has created a brave new world of science with a thousand machines to do his bidding. Yet he has no philosophical maturity to match it. His dependence on something be-

yond him thus becomes more acute because he gives it no conscious out-
let; he instinctively worships the computer. . . . science, man's new idol,
disclaims responsibility for ends and goals; it will not answer questions
that belong in the province of the spirit. At the same time it manages
to undermine the criteria by which man can decide moral or ethical
issues" (p. 212).

7. As Arthur Young points out in *The Reflexive Universe*, a growth-
oriented theory of evolution as compared to a Darwinian reduction-
istic theory, ". . . what has sustained us in [man's developmental]
climb? . . . it is sustained by the basic and most fundamental of all the
powers, the premonition of a goal implicit. . . . This premonition sustains the quest. It is the thrust, the passion that makes life continually
try to excel itself to evolve and, in almost all mankind, has led man to
postulate a state of being beyond himself. Religion does not induce the
belief. The belief is in our bones and blood and, when it so chooses,
gives sanction to religion. Religion, in fact, is its outward clothing, a
method of sharing and articulating the incomprehensible life force.
This brings us to the apparently paradoxical position of seeing religion
as the manifestation of physical and emotional, rather than spiritual,
causes" (p. 244).

8. Ferguson, Marilyn, *The Aquarian Conspiracy*. A well-organized
and intriguing cross-section of similar developments, across a broad variety of disciplines, in thinking/attitudes regarding the nature of man,
written by a highly respected scientific journalist.

9. Tabori, Paul, *Companions of the Unseen*. "It was known long before the Christian era that some persons possess special psychical faculties. The idea of mediumship is expressed clearly in the most ancient
writings, though the word medium is only about a hundred years old in
its present sense" (p. 28).

10. There are literally hundreds of books of varying quality on
psychic phenomena and research in these fields. The reader is advised to
use judgment in his selection of what to consider seriously. Thelma
Moss offers an excellent cross-section of solid references in her book
The Probability of the Impossible, as does Colin Wilson in his *Mysteries*. Jess Stearn is a very responsible journalist who has written several
books in this area. Perhaps the most widely known source of research
material in this country is the American Society for Psychical Research,
5 West 73rd St., New York, NY 10023. Samuel Weiser, Inc., 132 E.
24th St., New York, NY 10010 has an extensive selection of books and
references.

11. Unfortunately, psychic and physical phenomena presented in a nonscientific context are for the last sixty years or so received more as a theatrical event or entertainment than as providing meaningful data or information. H. P. Blavatsky, founder of the theosophical movement, had this to say regarding changing her focus of presentation from physical phenomena to verbal logic: "It was supposed that intelligent people, especially men of science, would at least have recognized the existence of a new and deeply interesting field of inquiry and research when they witnessed physical effects produced at will, for which they were not able to account. It was supposed that theologians would have welcomed the proof, of which they stand so sadly in need in these agnostic days, that the soul and the spirit are not mere creations of their fancy . . . but entities quite as real as the body, and much more important. These expectations were not realized. The phenomena were misunderstood and misrepresented, both as regards to their nature and their purpose. . . . The greater number of the witnesses developed an insatiable appetite for phenomena for their own sake, without any thought of studying the philosophy or the science of whose truth and power the phenomena were merely trivial, and so to say accidental illustration." (Quoted in *Reincarnation: The Phoenix Fire Mystery*, by Joseph Head and S. L. Cranston, p. 495.)

Regarding the phenomenon of physical materialization, Arthur Young in his book *The Reflexive Universe* cites Gustav Geley, *Clairvoyance and Materialization*, as follows: "During a trance a portion of [the medium's] organism is externalized . . . observation shows this ectoplasm as an amorphous substance which may be either solid or vaporous. Then, usually very soon, the formless substance becomes organic, it condenses, and forms appear, which, when the process is complete, have all the anatomical and physiological characters of biological life. The ectoplasm has become a living being or a fractional part of a living being. . . . This fact is substantiated, with formal proofs, by the common consent of scientists from all countries. . . . the phenomenon is the same in all countries, whoever the observer or the medium may be. Crookes, Gibiar, Sir Oliver Lodge, Professor Richet, Ochorowicz, Professor Moreselli, Dr. Imoda, Mme. Bisson, Dr. von Chrenk von Notzing, Crawford, Lebiedzinski, myself and others, all describe exactly the same thing" (p. 137; Galey, pp. 175–76).

A very pointed and poignant description of a reputable scientist struggling to integrate his scientific training and the evidence of his subjective experiences in controlled experiments with the trance medium Eusapia Palladino is described in *The Indefinite Boundary* by Guy L. Playfair.

12. Barham, Marti, *Bridging Two Worlds* (Merced, Calif.: MJB Books, 1981). MJB Books, Box 3246, Merced, CA 95344.

Chapter 1. The Soul, the Source, and the Three Universes

1. Tabori, Paul, *Companions of the Unseen*. "Some achievements of psychical research—for instance, experiments in telepathy—have as little mysticism about them as say electricity. We know just as little about some of the natural phenomena as about clairvoyance or thought transference. We still do not know what life, procreation, photosynthesis, or electricity are—though we can observe the manifestations, measure the effects and even reproduce them without having established the ultimate fundamental causes. Occultism is simply whatever cannot be fitted into 'official' science—sciences taught in schools and universities. Some 80 years ago hypnotism was something occult, today it is a subject of official medical science. . . . About 40 years ago Dr. Rudolph Tischner, a German psychic/researcher, wrote: 'Essentially we do not understand anything—we do not really understand the process of a billiard ball striking another and transferring its movements to it; we do not understand how our bodies actually grow; and least of all do we understand how the spirit affects the body and how we can move an arm or hand when we will it. But this lack of understanding is tempered to a certain extent because we have been able to classify a majority of facts in the world surrounding us—classify them under certain points of view and bring them into a systematic relationship to each other. The so-called occult facts are contrary to our systematic knowledge—in any case they cannot be coordinated easily within the generally accepted facts'" (p. 5).

2. The same holds true for many contemporary physicists, quite a few of which might be considered downright mystical in their view of the universe. Examples include Capra's *The Tao of Physics* and Pagels's *The Cosmic Code*. From the latter comes this sample statement: "Indeterminism was the first example of quantum weirdness. It implied the existence of physical events that were forever unknowable and unpredictable. Not only must human experimenters give up ever knowing when a particular atom is going to radiate or a particular nucleus undergo a radioactive decay, but these events are even unknown in the perfect mind of God. . . . Even God can give you only odds for some events to occur, not certainty" (p. 88).

Fritjof Capra is more than a "scientist." He is an experiencing human being. Check it out! Try telling him your "experiences"!

Regarding what man is now technically able to measure, and has yet to discover, Arthur Young in *The Reflexive Universe* points out that "Cosmology remains awe-inspiring despite efforts to wrap it up, and the moral is: don't trust the limited boundaries which the rational mind uses to protect itself. Don't permit statistical laws to give the illusion that there is nothing here but us chickens. In other words, don't conceal evidence, even the evidence for the potential divinity of man. According to Psalm 82 God said, 'Ye are gods and all of you are children of the most high.' "

3. Spragget, Allen, *The Unexplained*. "Man is a necessary expression of God. . . . The Universe would have no reason to exist without man to comprehend. . . . The universe was created for man and could not exist without man" (p. 126).

4. Revelation 11:6. "I am Alpha and Omega, the beginning and the end, the first and the last."

In his book *The Unobstructed Universe*, based on voice-channeled spiritual teachings, Stewart White makes the statement: "We must keep steadily in mind the realization that the supreme degree is beyond earth understanding actually, and that, while we here are privileged to examine all consciousness for the simple reason that we ourselves are individual bits of consciousness, and therefore within us is the *potential* capacity of understanding, we must do so from the finite aspect" (p. 106).

5. Pagels, Heinz, *Cosmic Code*. This contemporary theoretical physicist states: "Contrary to our impressions of the changeless heavens, the universe was and continues to be a place of great change" (p. 313).

6. Head, Joseph, and Cranston, S. L., *Reincarnation: The Phoenix Fire Mystery*. This is an excellent source of references for reincarnation beliefs/theories gleaned from many cultures over thousands of years. Unfortunately, the authors believe in the reward/punishment concept of karma, and some of their selections are undoubtedly colored by this attitude.

As Arthur Young in his book *The Reflexive Universe* states, ". . . if the soul is immortal, why then is a body mortal? It is because only the finite (or mortal) body is appropriate for learning. If the body were indestructible, it could not be injured and no learning could occur. This is the reason for mortality. . . . it is only by taking roles that the self learns to act, to achieve the competence required in order to have dominion over nature, to become, as Genesis puts it, 'as wise as gods, knowing good from evil'" (p. 253).

7. Darby and Joan, *Our Unseen Guest*. From this very readable and unpretentious presentation of voice-channeled spiritual teachings come the statements, "Supreme Consciousness (God) is the height of positiveness. . . . There can be nothing negative in the Supreme" (p. 270); "There is no actual evil just as there is no actual state of cold or actual state of total darkness. Cold is merely the absence of heat, darkness the absence of light. Evil is the non-development of good" (p. 283).

CHAPTER 2. THE UNOBSTRUCTED UNIVERSE

1. Adler, Mortimer J., *The Angels and Us*. Referring to human attempts to depict angels, this eminent philosopher says, "The imagery of dazzling, often blinding light also symbolizes the spirituality of angels. Pure spirits, totally incorporeal beings, cannot be painted, nor can they be described in words that call images to mind. Only by using the symbolism of light, which makes the invisible visible, can painters and poets try to prevent an egregious misunderstanding of the imagery that they are compelled to employ. The bodily forms and features that they depict angels as having must be recognized as pictorial metaphors, not as literal representations of what angels are like."

Darby and Joan, *Our Unseen Guest*. "'My present body has properties beyond your comprehension, such as color beyond the humanly visible spectrum.'"

2. Adler, *The Angels and Us*. "According to the theologian, angels speak to God, but only in the sense that they communicate their receptivity of their will to God's grace and the obedience of their will to God's law." According to Adler's historical survey, distance involved in angelic communication poses no problem. "Since heaven is not a physical place, the members of the angelic society who communicate with one another there are not separated from one another by spatial distances."

3. Adler, *The Angels and Us*. "In their local motion, angels sometimes move like the massive bodies in Isaac Newton's celestial mechanics—going from place to place by passing through all the points in the intervening space and requiring a span of time to do so. But they

also sometimes move like the electrons in Niels Bohr's early version of quantum mechanics—transferring the exertion of their spiritual power over a body in one place to a body in another by doing so instantaneously and without passing through all the points in the space between the two bodies. . . . The theologians tell us that when angelic motion from place to place is not instantaneous, the duration of the motion is not a measurable span of physical time. So, too, when the local motion of an angel is continuous rather than discontinuous, the translation of its spiritual power from one place to another is not the same as the passage of a body through the space that intervenes between one place and another'' (p. 132).

4. Head, Joseph, and Cranston, S. L., *Reincarnation: The Phoenix Fire Mystery*. Gustav Stromberg, an astronomer and physicist interested in the correlation of many natural physical events with subjective human experience and the ultimate meaning of life, presented some of his findings and interpretations in a variety of works. Albert Einstein was apparently particularly impressed with one of his works (*The Soul of the Universe*) and what Einstein considered "the successful attempt to pick out of the bewildering variety of researches that which is of essential value, and to present it in such a way that the concept of Oneness of all can for the first time be stated with definite intent." From this work Head and Cranston cite the following statement: "Our memories are indelibly 'engraved' in our brain field, that is, the electrical field which determines the structures and functions of our brain. By analogy we conclude that our brain field and the 'memory genie' associated with it, contract in unchanged form [at death] and disappear from the physical world, that is, the world of matter, radiation, and force fields. Where does the brain field go to? Presumably it goes back to the same world from which it originally came. Since it no longer has any size, or at least any definable size, its properties cannot be described in the language used in the science of physics. In other words, it disappears into a nonphysical world." Further on he says, "There are, therefore, good reasons for making the following important assertion: a soul is indestructible and immortal. It carries an indelible record of all its activities." In a later work titled *The Searchers*, apparently elaborating his thoughts in novel form, he makes the following comments: "Our real selves, our souls, belong before our birth, during our organic life, and after our death to the non-physical world. All the memories of our last and previous lives can be reviewed [there] in full details in an instant, since there are no atoms, which in the physical world block and slow down all our mental activities. . . . The atoms form a screen or veil that

makes it possible for us to concentrate on the immediate requirements of our earthly life. When this veil disappears at death, our memories from this and perhaps earlier lives crowd in upon us without hindrance" (pp. 422, 423).

5. Edmunds, I. G., *Other Lives: The Story of Reincarnation*. This book has some good references, including religious writings that the author relates to the idea of reincarnation. Concerning contemporary and historical Western religious attitudes towards reincarnation, Edmunds says, "According to both religions [Judaism and Christianity] people have but one chance to redeem themselves of their sins. If they fail to do this in their lifetime, the opportunity is lost forever. Many religionists say this is a good thing. If we have other lives in which we can correct and redeem the sins of this one then there is no pressure upon people to be just, devout, and God-fearing in their present lives. There is danger of people saying 'we can atone in a later life'" (p. 90).

6. Despite apparent rejection by most Christian religions and much of orthodox Judaism, the concept of, and belief in, reincarnation is found in many other world religions both contemporary and ancient. Much has been written about this subject by many serious religious teachers and philosophers for hundreds of years, and it is far beyond the scope of this book to attempt any survey of the arguments and variations. A sample of a few eminent people from the great variety of cultural, religious, and vocational dimensions who have either endorsed or seriously considered the concept includes: Buddha, Hermes, Origen, Albert Schweitzer, Pythagoras, Herodotus, Socrates, Plato, Aristotle, Plotinus, Shakespeare, Milton, Voltaire, Benjamin Franklin, Blake, Wordsworth, Shelley, Emerson, Thoreau, Whitman, Tolstoy, Arthur Conan Doyle, Gustav Mahler, Henry Ford, Rudyard Kipling, Jean Sibelius, W. B. Yeats, Kahlil Gibran, Thomas Edison, William James, Carl Jung, Nietzsche, Gandhi, Sai Baba.

7. Sugrue, Thomas, *There Is a River*. This respected chronicler of the life and work of Edgar Cayce speaks of people wanting to use the concept of karma in an inappropriate sense regarding their readings with Cayce. "People almost invariably got the wrong idea about their life readings. If a man were told that he had once, as another personality, been rich and powerful, he was inclined to be content with his present mediocrity and regard his past as an inheritance he had just come into. If a woman were told that she had once been glamorous and irresistible she was inclined to relax smugly, overlooking her present obesity and lack of charm. . . . There was a tendency also to regard the soul as a

permanent personality. People would say, 'I was so and so, in my last appearance, I was in England.' When Edgar tried to combat this notion by saying that each personality of a soul was a separate experience, in no way related to other experiences of the soul except by common inclusion in a large enterprise, he found the going heavy, especially with the ladies . . . '' (p. 278).

8. In *Reincarnation: The Phoenix Fire Mystery*, physicist R. C. Johnson is quoted (from his book *A Religious Outlook for Modern Man*) as follows: "The permanent soul which stores the wisdom, goodness, artistic sensitivity, interests and skills of the past, surely influences in some degree the new personality which it is sending forth into the world. Normally, we should expect some of these interests or capacities to awaken as the child develops. Some may remain wholly latent, for a soul's desire is to broaden its experience rather than to intensify certain aspects of it. Plato has a theory that the kind of knowledge which comes easily is 'old' knowledge in the sense that we have laid foundations for it in prior lives, while the learning in which at first we find little interest or which presents difficulty is probably being met for the first time."

9. It is curious how the concept of karma has gradually changed through the years to a focus on reward or punishment rather than the broader outlook of learning how to balance and integrate one's life. H. P. Blavatsky, founder of theosophy and certainly knowledgeable about karmic beliefs the world over, speaks of the concept in the sense of harmony in *The Secret Doctrine*. As cited in *Reincarnation: The Phoenix Fire Mystery*, she says, "For the only decree of karma—an eternal and immutable decree—is absolute harmony in the world of matter as it is in the world of spirit. It is not therefore karma that rewards or punishes but it is we who reward or punish ourselves according to whether we work with, through and along with nature, abiding by the laws on which that harmony depends, or break them . . ." (p. 520).

10. Adler, *The Angels and Us*. Adler makes a comment concerning the heavenly community of angels: "It is a society of perfect concord and flawless peace. . . . In the second place, it is a society in which the divine law that governs it need not be accompanied by coercive force. Angelic obedience to the precepts of divine law is an indefectible response, flowing naturally from the goodness of the angelic will, and also supernaturally from the charity that is a gift of God's grace" (p. 140).

11. Adler, *The Angels and Us*. "The action of angels on earth and in relation to human beings is, in fact, performed only by some angels, not

by all, not even by most. In the main, the life of angels—of all angels, even those who carry messages to mankind or have earthly missions to perform—consists in what they do in heaven, not what they do on earth" (p. 69).

CHAPTER 3. THE OBSTRUCTED UNIVERSE: PHYSICAL/SPIRITUAL BEINGS

1. Beebe-Hill, Ruth, *Hanta-Yo*. This documentary novel of the life philosophy of American Indians prior to contact with the white man includes a number of spiritual teachings compatible with information gained in our own darkroom experiences. A sample extract appropriate to not denying one's physical needs: "Live in the Spirit, say the grandfathers; the Spirit never will demand a surrender of your reason or deny you any urge. Whoever says that man shall suspend his reasoning looks for ways of stifling the Spirit, and whoever says that man shall repress his natural desires hunts ways for killing joy. . . . Appreciate yourself, the grandfathers say. . . . Use your body for giving growth to the spirit, your spirit . . . you, who shall become the Great Spirit" (p. 576).

2. Beebe-Hill, *Hanta-Yo*. "Man arrives on earth owning a visible body and a competitive spirit. Observe the child, the youth; he honors this spirit in his young seasons, the people recognizing his zest for rivalry . . . for contest . . . as a way of keeping true to self. . . . But the spirit, slow growing, begins to seek repose. And so the same warrior, ever loyal to self, accepts the demands of an expanding spirit. The people call this growth, wisdom; a wise man, a man loyal to his spiritual growth, a man truly stable" (p. 705).

As Stewart White points out in *The Unobstructed Universe*, the entities he was in contact with via voice-channeling stated that there was "no stability to 'spiritual development' unless first a foundation had been established for it by adequate accomplishment of the ordinary things of the life in which we find ourselves. We may think we are making progress for eternity by 'withdrawing ourselves from the sordidness of life.' We may imagine we are getting somewhere by cultivating assiduously our 'higher nature,' either by our own inner meditations, or by following the practices of some religion or cult. And, indeed, we may gain by such conscious effort—but only if we have first done thoroughly and adequately the ordinary commonplace job of living out what is thrust under our noses. That is what we are here for. And it makes no great matter how sincere are our 'higher' intentions.'' As the voice-channel entity stated, "You make a cult out of service . . . you have eliminated service, and created nothing but egoistic satisfaction. And egoistic satisfaction is a straight road to self-adulation, and that leads to attempted dictatorship'' (pp. 242–43). The channeled entity continues in the same vein when she states: "There has been too much holier-than-thou stuff, and not enough recognition of the genuine adequacy of growth'' (p. 244).

3. The Holy Bible, Lamsa edition, 1 Corinthians 15:37. "And what you sow is not the body that shall be, but the bare grain; it may chance to be wheat or barley or some other seed. . . . 15:38: "But God gives it a body as it has pleased Him, and to every seed, its own natural body.''

4. The English psychic Matthew Manning received a channeled message from his grandfather who had recently died; the grandfather's description of being above the ground and seeing his body on the ground includes the following: "Next I saw a silvery cord from my body to the new entity. This cord extended from my shoulders, at the base of my head'' (*The Link*, p. 123). A Bible reference sometimes referred to in this connection is Ecclesiastes 12:6–7: "Remember him before the silver cord is cut off and the golden bowl is broken and the pitcher is broken at the fountain or the wheel is broken at the cistern, then the dust shall return to the earth as it was; and the spirit shall return to God who gave it.'' However, while many writers have used Bible references either to support or to deny psychic/spiritual events, this may essentially be an exercise in futility. As I. G. Edmunds says in *Other Lives: The Story of Reincarnation*, "Many passages in the Bible are written in such a way that one person could understand it in one way and another person would see the meaning in the exactly opposite way'' (p. 90).

5. Bible, Lamsa ed., Ecclesiastes 1:11. "There is no remembrance of former generations; neither shall there be any remembrance of generations that are to come with those that will come after.''

Mohandas Gandhi, in a letter to a close friend and follower of his teachings, had this to say regarding not remembering previous life events: "What you say about rebirth is sound. It is nature's kindness that we do not remember past births. Where is the good either of knowing in detail the numberless births we have gone through? Life would be a burden if we carried such a tremendous load of memory. A wise man deliberately forgets many things, even as a lawyer forgets the cases and their details as soon as they are disposed of. Yes, 'Death is but a sleep and a forgetting'" (from Joseph Head and S. L. Cranston, *Reincarnation: The Phoenix Fire Mystery*, p. 476).

6. Darby and Joan, *Our Unseen Guest*. In a letter that the discarnate entity Steven dictates to Darby and Joan, he says, "Fear is the greatest enemy of the human mind. It causes more suffering than any other one thing. Yes, the banishing of fear is what I want to do for others besides yourselves; this is why in the hour of earth's hideousness, I was allowed to tell you these truths." He closes by saying, "I am your friend, I shall always be with you, and if you will, be with me" (p. 319).

CHAPTER 4. THE OBSTRUCTED UNIVERSE: STRUGGLING FOR MATURITY

1. Concerning the magnitude of issues we are to learn, Gandhi offers the following perspective. "If for mastery of the physical sciences you have to devote a whole life time, how many life times may be needed for mastering the greatest spiritual force that mankind has known? For if this is the only permanent thing in life, if this is the only thing that counts, then whatever effort you bestow on mastering it is well spent."

CHAPTER 5. THE OBSTRUCTED UNIVERSE: PSYCHIC/SPIRITUAL INFLUENCES

1. Darby and Joan, *Our Unseen Guest*. "The free will of man, my dear sir, is the one attribute that is wholly and distinctly his own. . . . Animal life does not have free will . . . this is man's peculiar possession. Because of free will man is man. Not to use the freedom of one's will is to deny oneself of self. Free will constitutes every man's opportunity, permitting him to control the degree of consciousness he attains on graduation. . . . As to the purpose of free will, make no mistake. For it is only as the free will carries out the behest of that still small voice, man's quality of consciousness, that the lessons of earth are finished, the book closed and a wider world, a greater freedom and more perfect understanding attained upon graduation. . . . Do not make any mistake about the freedom of man's will. It is his to use and use develops it, just as exercise develops the muscles of one's body. Disuse deadens it" (pp. 275, 276).

2. Tabori, Paul, *Companions of the Unseen.* "Occult originally meant nothing more than hidden, not understood, not experienced. Modern dictionaries define it as supernatural, magical, secret, esoteric —but at the dawn of civilization almost every process of nature belonged in this category. Ignorance was almost boundless. Radioactivity, hypnosis, infrared and ultra-violet rays, television, antibiotics, these are only a few examples of recent achievements which in the past centuries would have been called witchcraft" (p. 3).

3. Spragget, Allen, *The Unexplained.* This well-referenced and documented collection of historical data and the author's own speculations/experiences offers a very solid general reading source for psychic/spiritual phenomena. Concerning the phenomenon of spiritual healing he quotes Katherine Kuhlman, a widely recognized healer: "I have nothing to do with the healing, the miracles are produced by the power of God. And you can't analyze God's power anymore than you can analyze God. I am utterly dependent on the mercy and compassion of God." Spragget describes her attitude towards her healing services as seeming to reflect "perfect innocence, faith in an all loving and all powerful father" (p. 167). In expanding on the experience of Kuhlman as going into an altered state of consciousness—an experience also reported by many other healers and psychics—Spragget elaborates some aspects of the experience and compares them to identified psychological states. "None of the psychoanalytic or parapsychological arguments are able to explain the Kuhlman healings. Nor can they duplicate them. . . . Psychological vivisection can only go so far. It cannot lay bare the inscrutable something in Katherine Kuhlman that makes her a channel for healing. It can give us hints, that's all. . . . In her healing work we are up against the ultimate mystery. In fact, there is a kind of psychological 'uncertainty principle' involved. The more you rationally analyze the healing power, the farther away from it you get. You can understand it (approximately anyway), but not be able to use it. Or you can use it, but not be able to understand it" (p. 180). Alex Holmes, recognized with Harry Edwards as one of England's most successful and popular healers, offered the following comment on the inconsistency of healing results: "I can't explain that. But I am quite sure that in many cases it comes back to my own lack of faith. I remember the case of a spastic boy . . . he seemed ready for it . . . on the verge of healing . . . but as I prayed for his legs, a great doubt came into my mind. I was unable to help that boy. He was ready, but I wasn't. This is something that is liable to happen to any of us. A great deal depends on

our spiritual condition. We must always strive to keep in touch with God, to be an open channel."

4. Spragget, *The Unexplained*. The psychoanalyst N. Fodor, long a serious investigator into things psychic/spiritual, is quoted as having reached similar conclusions: "I think that these cases of alleged possession are explainable on purely psychoanalytic grounds. What is involved is possession by an idea, and personality embodies ideas. Spirit possession is probably nothing more than neurosis or borderline psychosis. . . . It is a very dangerous field and risky to utter an opinion. You would need tremendous evidence to support the theory [of possession]. I have never found any cases, although I have investigated a few instances of purported possession. On the other hand, in my psychoanalytic work I have treated many individuals with similar beliefs from a psychological point of view" (p. 206).

5. Spragget, *The Unexplained*. In discussing fraud in psychic and spiritual matters, Spragett makes this interesting statement: "I believe it is highly probable that genuine physical mediumship does exist. Fraud seems pointless unless there is something genuine to simulate. Materialization, apports, levitations, direct voice, these and other equally astounding phenomena have been attested to by reputable witnesses including some of the great minds of their day." He then lists a number of prominent scientists, including Nobel Prize winner Charles Richet (p. 97).

Swan, Ingo, *To Kiss Earth Goodbye*. In a work well indexed and referenced, this recognized psychic describes some of his own theories and experiences and refers to some historical events related to religious figures. The seventeenth-century monk Josef Cupertino was seen over a period of years to levitate at will. A cardinal who later became pope "examined this case of levitation and felt inspired to pronounce it real." Josef was later declared a saint. St. Thomas Aquinas is said to have floated in religious ecstasy. St. Theresa was said often to rise from the floor before her astonished Carmelite sisters (p. 79).

Spragget, *The Unexplained*. N. Fodor states: "At the bottom of the human mind, or I would rather call it the organismic mind, there are electromagnetic powers of which we know nothing, but the capabilities of which we may suspect in the way in which they build the human body according to an amazing blueprint. . . . The biologists speak of an organizer, a kind of engineer which supervises the body-building in the womb" (p. 208).

6. Roberts, Jane, *Seth Speaks*; also *The Seth Material*.

7. Darby and Joan, *Our Unseen Guest*. "What actually happens during the process of [psychic] communication is more like the transmission of a wireless message than anything else in your experience. Our term receiving station is very good, not because it is metaphorical but because it is the exact opposite of metaphorical. . . . I communicate by means of a medium which is quite material. I utilize a force which man does not now understand, but which in time he will. A few years ago men marveled at the ordinary telegraph, now they are reconciled to wireless." (This book was originally written in 1920.)

8. Spragget, *The Unexplained*. Spragget speaks of "secondary personalities," a phenomenon known to psychology, as possibly similar to the trance personality. "A spirit control is not necessarily supernormal but may be merely abnormal, a secondary personality of the medium. This would not imply play-acting or faking by the medium. A secondary personality is not a conscious impersonation but an autonomous self with a psychic life of its own. However, there are differences as well as similarities between a mediumistic trance personality and the typical case of multiple personalities in the records of psychopathology. In the first place, the trance personality is in one sense under the control of the medium's conscious mind; as a rule it manifests only at the summons of the medium. This is not true of the multiple personality, which comes 'out' at will, independent of the wishes of the normal self. . . . Moreover, the spiritualist guide represents a high moral code and generally has an elevating effect on the medium's ethical life. The multiple personality, on the other hand, often is morally deficient and sometimes drags the body into acts that the normal self would shun. This spirit control is considered an asset by the typical medium, a spiritual blessing and guidance. The victim of multiple personality invariably regards his second self as a liability, a demon to be exorcised. . . . And last, the mediumistic trance personality characteristically possesses powerful ESP, while the standard secondary personality is not noted for this" (pp. 66, 67).

9. Darby and Joan, *Our Unseen Guest*. Some trance mediums refer to interference by the medium's personality as coloring. "In mental communication the receiving station must constantly differentiate between their own thoughts and those of the communicator; failure to so differentiate results in coloring. . . . Coloring results when the conscious mind of the receiving station overrules the subconscious. Suppose I

started to give you a name [using the Ouija board]. *Mar* I spell. By the time I get that far, Joan's conscious mind may have supplied the letter *y* because one who is with her much is named Mary. Now the name I try to give might have been Martha, Marian, Marie, Maria, Marietta, etc.'' This channeled voice also refers to what he calls cross-currents— messages coming through from other connections, just as a "wireless station often picks up messages not intended for it. . . . These cross-currents are unavoidable, and the coloring caused is quite as annoying to us as to you" (p. 80).

10. Darby and Joan, *Our Unseen Guest*. "Remember that the will, the act, is yours. What would it profit a man if, with his steps charted out for him one by one he followed them blindly, granted Supremacy itself has made the chart? The individual consciousness must vision its own future and choose itself when to work on future" (p. 82). "Deny the freedom of a man's will and immediately you have denied man's very being. Man in truth can be defined only in terms of free will. . . . It is because your wills are free that fortune telling is futile. Except as I judge of your quality I do not know what you, and the freedom of your will, will do tomorrow. . . . You can study the causes at work in a given situation and with more or less accuracy predict the effect that will result from those causes. So do we here, though our more complete knowledge gives us greater accuracy of foresight. In Supremacy (God) the scroll is quite unrolled. Knowing all, Supremacy can foresee all. But Supremacy knowledge of the will-be is founded on understanding of was and is. The parallel between prevision on my plane and on yours holds even in the Supreme degree" (p. 281).

11. Fox, Oliver, *Astral Projection*; Crookall, Robert, *The Study and Practice of Astral Projection*; Monroe, Robert, *Journeys Out of the Body*.

Chapter 6. Look Homeward, Angel

1. Aries, Phillippe, *The Hour of Our Death*. Prior to the influence of the Christian religion, death was much more an accepted part of life and generally included a positive submission to the inevitability of death as well as the healthy expression of natural emotions. Genuine premonitions of one's own death are said to have occurred much more frequently then. Aries refers to such an attitude as a "tame death."

Contemporary attitudes, believed to have been heavily influenced by Christianity, he refers to as having resulted in a "wild death." The concepts of hell and damnation are seen as interfering with acceptance of death and thereby creating unnecessary fright and pain.

2. Tatelbaum, Judy, *The Courage to Grieve*. Kübler-Ross, Elizabeth, *Death: The Final Stage of Growth*.

3. Sabom, Michael, *Recollections of Death: A Medical Investigation*. Throwing out "contaminated" data and sticking to clearly defined medical near-death criteria, Sabom found 43 percent of subjects reported one or more aspects of a subjective near-death experience following a *medical* near-death event. "From this, we can say that the NDE is a common experience among persons surviving an episode of unconsciousness and near death" (p. 57).

4. Gallup, George, and Proctor, William, *Adventures in Immortality*. "The impression of reviewing or reexamining the individual's past life in a brief, highly compressed period of time was a solid 11 percent of those we polled, or more than two and one-half million people of the total population" (p. 32).

5. Sabom, *Recollections of Death*. Sabom cites Wilder Penfield, the late internationally famous neurosurgeon and researcher in mapping brain activity, who ended up with a dualistic conclusion regarding mind and body. He quotes Penfield as saying, "For myself, after a professional lifetime of trying to discover how the brain accounts for the mind, it comes as a surprise now to discover, during this final examination of the evidence, that the dualists' hypothesis (separation of mind and brain) seems the more reasonable of the two possible explanations. . . . Mind comes into action and goes out of action with the highest brain mechanism, it is true. But mind has energy. The form of the energy is different from that of neuronal potentials that travel the axon pathways. There I must leave it" (p. 83).

Sabom, *Recollections of Death*. Sabom seems to be leaning towards a conclusion similar to Penfield's when he says, "Since I suspect that the NDE is a reflection of a mind-brain split, I cannot help but wonder why such an event should occur at the point of near-death. Could the mind which splits apart from the physical brain be, in essence, the soul, which continues to exist after final bodily death, according to some religious doctrines? . . . As I see it, this is the ultimate question that has been raised by reports of the NDE. It is here at the point of near-death, that scientific facts and theories interface with religious doctrines and speculations'' (p. 185).

6. Darby and Joan, *Our Unseen Guest*. In regard to being greeted after the transition of physical death, the channeled entity Stephen makes a comparison to a nurse greeting someone after an operation: "Haven't I told you that some of us will be on hand to hold your hand and persuade you that really the operation is over and that, after all, it didn't kill you?" (p. 230).

7. Spragget, Allen, *The Unexplained*. "Creation has been going on forever, continues, and will go on forever. . . . There is work for all to do" (p. 127).

Spragget, *The Unexplained*. Concerning the purpose of life of each person, S. Fodor said, "Human life is bigger than we know. In fact, we have no idea just how big it is. It would appear that we are here in a kindergarten, really, for the purpose of growing. . . . I don't think that happiness or unhappiness is the purpose of human life. The purpose is growth. And in order to grow we must be gregarious, we must be of service to others. Growth and service, actually these are the two fundamental principles of human life. . . . I think this growth will continue after physical death for it is a fundamental universal process. Evolution itself is nothing but the principle of growth. . . . When we leave this kindergarten of life, we continue to grow."

Bibliography

Adler, Mortimer J., *The Angels and Us* (New York: MacMillan, 1982).

Aries, Phillippe, *The Hour of Our Death* (New York: Knopf, 1981).

Barham, Marti, *Bridging Two Worlds* (Merced, Calif.: MJB Books, 1981).

Beebe-Hill, Ruth, *Hanta-Yo* (Garden City, N. Y.: Doubleday & Co., 1979).

Bentov, Itzhak, *Stalking the Wild Pendulum* (New York: Dutton, 1977).

Capra, Fritjof, *The Tao of Physics* (New York: Random House, 1980).

Cerminara, Gina, *Many Mansions* (New York: New American Library, 1967).

Crookall, Robert, *The Study & Practice of Astral Projection* (Secaucus, N.J.: University Books, 1966).

Crooks, W., *Researches in the Phenomenon of Spiritualism* (London: Psychic Book Club, 1874/1953).

Darby & Joan, *Our Unseen Guest* (New York: Harper & Bros., 1920).

Ebon, Martin, *They Knew the Unknown* (New York: World Publishing, 1971).

Edmunds, I. G., *Other Lives: The Story of Reincarnation* (New York: McGraw-Hill, 1979).

Fielding, E.; Baggally, W. W.; and Corrington, H., "Report on a series of sittings with Eusapia Palladino," *Proceedings of the Society for Psychical Research*, vol. 23, pt. 59, p. 569. (Reported in *The Indefinite Boundary*, by G. L. Playfair.)

Eisenbud, Jules, *The World of Ted Serios* (New York: Morrow, 1967).

Fox, Oliver, *Astral Projection* (Seacaucus, N.J.: Citadel Press, 1979).

Ferguson, Marilyn, *The Aquarian Conspiracy* (Los Angeles: Tarcher, 1980).

Gallup, George, and Proctor, William, *Adventures in Immortality* (New York: McGraw-Hill, 1982).

Garrett, Eileen J., *Does Man Survive Death?* (New York: Helix Press, 1957).

Geley, Gustav, *Clairvoyance and Materialization* (London: Allen & Unwin, 1927).

Graves, Tom, and Hoult, Janet, *The Essential T. C. Lethbridge.* (London: Routledge & Kegan Paul, 1980).

Head, Joseph, and Cranston, S. L., *Reincarnation: The Phoenix Fire Mystery* (New York: Julian Press/Crown Publishers, 1977).

Koestler, Arthur, *The Roots of Coincidence* (New York: Random House, 1972).

Kraft, Dean, *Portrait of a Psychic Healer* (New York: G. P. Putnam & Sons, 1981).

Kübler-Ross, Elizabeth, *Death: The Final Stage of Growth* (Englewood Cliffs, N. J.: Prentice-Hall, 1975).

Lamsa, George M., *The Holy Bible from Ancient Eastern Manuscripts* (San Francisco: Harper & Row, 1933).

LeShan, Lawrence, *The Medium, The Mystic & The Physicist* (New York: Ballantine Books, 1975).

Lorimer, David, *Survival? Body, Mind and Death in the Light of Psychic Experience* (London: Routledge & Kegan Paul, 1984).

Manning, Matthew, *The Link* (New York: Holt, Rinehart & Winston, 1975).

Monroe, Robert A., *Journeys Out of the Body* (Garden City, N. Y.: Anchor Books, 1977).

Moody, Raymond R., *Life After Life* (New York: Bantam Books, 1976).

Moss, Thelma, *The Probability of the Impossible* (New York: Plume Books, N. A. L., 1974).

Murphy, Gardner, and Ballou, Robert O., *William James on Psychical Research* (New York: Viking, 1960).

Osis, Karlis, and Haraldsson, Erlendur, *At the Hour of Death* (New York: Avon, 1977).

Ostrander, Sheila, and Schroeder, Lynn, *Psychic Discoveries behind the Iron Curtain* (Englewood Cliffs, N. J.: Prentice-Hall, 1970).

Pagels, Heinz, *The Cosmic Code: Quantum Physics as the Language of Nature* (New York: Simon & Schuster, 1982).

Playfair, Guy L., *The Indefinite Boundary* (New York: St. Martins Press, 1976).

Ring, Kenneth, *Life at Death* (New York: Coward, McCann & Geoghegan, 1980).

Sabom, Michael B., *Recollections of Death: A Medical Investigation* (New York: Harper & Row, 1982).

Spragget, Allen, *The Unexplained* (New York: New American Library, 1967).

Stearn, Jess, *A Matter of Immortality* (New York: Atheneum, 1976).

Stearn, Jess, *Adventures into the Psychic* (New York: Signet, 1971).

Stevenson, Ian, "Twenty Cases Suggestive of Reincarnation," Proceedings of the American Society for Psychical Research, vol. 26 (1966), pp. 1–362.

Sugrue, Thomas, *There Is a River* (New York: Holt, 1945).

Swan, Ingo, *To Kiss Earth Goodbye* (New York: Hawthorn Books, 1975).

Tabori, Paul, *Companions of the Unseen* (New Hyde Park, N. Y.: University Books, 1968).

Tanous, Alex, *Beyond Coincidence* (Garden City, N. Y.: Doubleday, 1976).

Tatelbaum, Judy, *The Courage to Grieve* (San Francisco: Harper & Row, 1980).

White, Stewart Edward, *The Unobstructed Universe* (New York: E. P. Dutton & Co., 1940). Excellent!

Wilson, Colin, *Mysteries* (New York: Putnam's, 1978).

Young, Arthur M., *The Reflexive Universe* (Delacorte Press/Seymour Lawrence, 1976).